A bumpy recovery amid continued threat of COVID-19

- The global economy continues to struggle from the impact of the coronavirus disease (COVID-19) pandemic. While some economies have rebounded in the third quarter of 2020, the continued threat of COVID-19 remains the primary concern, with governments reinstating partial containment measures to deal with new outbreaks in certain areas. The latest forecast is for a 4.4% global contraction in 2020 but for a recovery in 2021 with growth of 5.2%. The economy of developing Asia is expected to contract by 0.7% in 2020, the first regional recession in almost 6 decades. It is projected to post a 6.8% recovery in 2021, slower than the pre–COVID-19 forecast. Risks to the outlook are on the downside, depending heavily on the speed of resolving the pandemic as well as the extent of global spillovers from a weakened external sector.

- The Pacific subregion reels as the pandemic devastates its economies, which rely mostly on the external sector. From the 4.3% decline forecast in July 2020, the subregional gross domestic product (GDP) forecast for 2020 has been further downgraded. The two largest economies in the Pacific—Papua New Guinea and Fiji—are expected to suffer worse than previously forecasted. With travel bans and different forms of containment measures still in place, other tourism-dependent countries such as the Cook Islands, Niue, Palau, and Vanuatu struggle to prop up their economies. Meanwhile, smaller economies that depend on imported basic commodities are suffering from bottlenecks brought about by the pandemic. The subregion is expected to recover and grow by 1.3% in 2021, contingent on how quickly travel and trade restrictions are lifted.

- The United States bounced back in the third quarter of 2020 as the economy grew at an annualized rate of 33.1%. The jump came after a 31.4% contraction in the previous quarter as many states across the country implemented containment measures to stem the spread of the virus. Higher consumption, together with advances in business and residential investment as well as exports, drove the recovery. Nevertheless, risks remain on the downside as the number of COVID-19 cases increases. The full-year 2020 forecast remains unchanged, with the United States economy expected to contract by 5.3%. However, the 2021 recovery now appears to be slightly faster at 4.0% compared with the earlier forecast of 3.8%.

- After contracting by 6.8% year-on-year (y-o-y) in the first quarter, the People's Republic of China recovered strongly, posting 3.2% growth in the second quarter, followed by 4.9% in the third quarter. Broad-based growth was observed in most sectors, with the manufacturing, mining, and utilities sectors growing the fastest at 6.0% in the third quarter from a year earlier. While the services sector is expected to recover further, weak domestic consumption and external sector will continue to dampen recovery. The economy of the People's Republic of China is forecast to grow by 1.8% in 2020 and accelerate to 7.7% in 2021.

- After three quarters of recession, Japan's economy exited recession as it posted an annualized growth of 21.4% in the third quarter of 2020 led by higher domestic and external demand. Although this exceeded expectations, the economy is still 6.0% smaller than it was a year ago. A 4.7% growth in private consumption was recorded as households spent more on cars, leisure, and restaurants; and overseas demand pushed exports up by 7.0%. Despite this, the full-year 2020 projected contraction for Japan's economy has been further downgraded to 5.4% from the initial forecast of a 5.0% contraction. Expected growth in 2021 remains at 2.0%.

- The Australian economy plunged into a recession after its GDP shrank by 7.0% in the second quarter of 2020. The combined impact of the pandemic and government containment measures led to large drops across several economic

Gross Domestic Product Growth (%, annual)

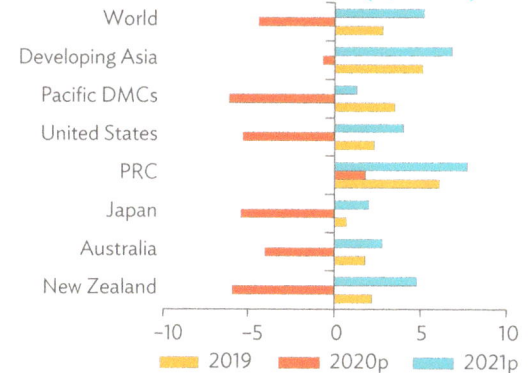

ADB = Asian Development Bank, DMC = developing member country, GDP = gross domestic product, p = projection, PRC = People's Republic of China.
Notes: Developing Asia and Pacific DMCs as defined by ADB. Figures are based on ADB estimates except for world GDP growth.
Sources: ADB. 2020. *Asian Development Outlook 2020 Update: Wellness in Worrying Times.* Manila; International Monetary Fund. 2020. *World Economic Outlook October 2020: A Long and Difficult Ascent.* Washington, DC.

Gross Domestic Product Growth in Developing Asia (%, annual)

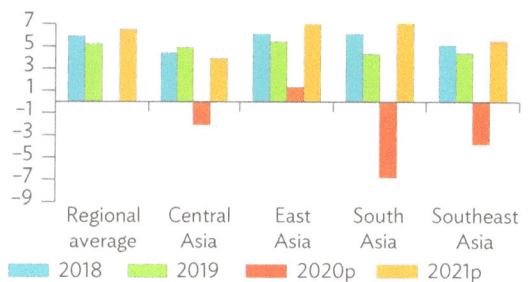

p = projection.
Source: Asian Development Bank. 2020. *Asian Development Outlook 2020 Update: Wellness in Worrying Times.* Manila.

COVID-19 Cases in Pacific DMCs

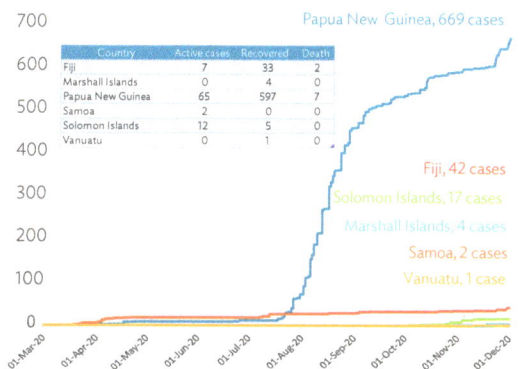

COVID-19 = coronavirus disease, DMC = developing member country.
Note: Data as of 1 December 2020.
Sources: M. Roser, H. Ritchie, E. Ortiz-Ospina, and J. Hasell. 2020. *Coronavirus Pandemic (COVID-19).* Published online at OurWorldInData.org. Retrieved from: https://ourworldindata.org/coronavirus; Worldometer COVID-19 Data.

Average Spot Price of Brent Crude Oil
(monthly, $/bbl)

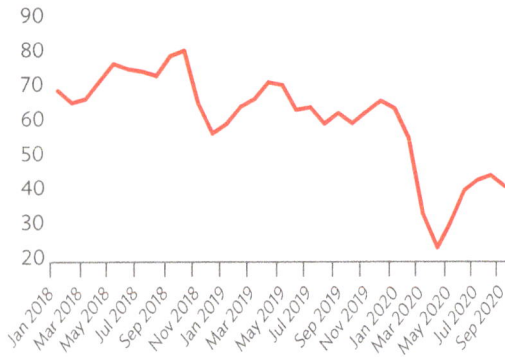

$/bbl = dollars per barrel.
Source: World Bank Commodity Price Data (Pink Sheet).

Price of Export Commodities
(2018 = 100, annual)

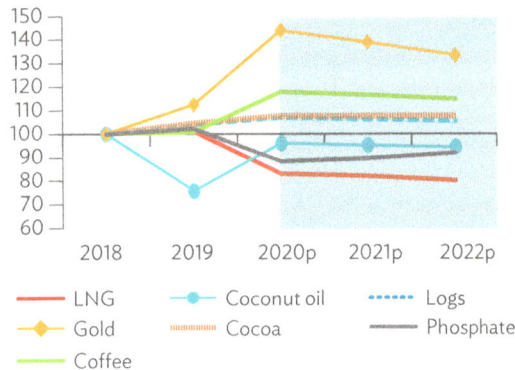

LNG —— Coconut oil —— Logs ......
Gold —— Cocoa —— Phosphate ——
Coffee ——

LNG = liquefied natural gas, p = projection.
Source: Asian Development Bank calculations using data from World Bank Commodity Price Data (Pink Sheets).

Tourist Departures Bound for Pacific Destinations
('000 persons, January–August totals)

Australia   New Zealand

Sources: Australian Bureau of Statistics and Statistics New Zealand.

Lead authors: Noel Del Castillo and Rommel Rabanal

aggregates. Closures of hotels, restaurants, and other services because of the pandemic resulted in more than 12.0% drop in household consumption and almost 18.0% fall in spending on services. The outlook remains uncertain over concerns of possible succeeding waves of the virus outbreak. The Consensus Forecast for 2020 is a contraction of 4.0% in 2020 and growth of 2.8% in 2021.

- New Zealand's economy posted its deepest recession yet, with GDP contracting by 12.2% in the second quarter of 2020. The nationwide lockdown, implemented by the government to contain the pandemic, paralyzed business activity. Widespread declines have been recorded across indicators. Household spending declined by 12.1% with major declines in spending on services, e.g., restaurant meals, ready-to-eat food, domestic air passenger services, and recreation and cultural activities. Meanwhile, investment spending fell by 20.8% because of less construction, as well as reduced investments in plant, machinery, and equipment. The Consensus Forecast projects the economy to shrink by 5.9% in 2020 and recover by 4.8% the following year.

Mixed prospects for commodity prices as COVID-19 remains a major risk

- Some commodity prices are starting to rise again, while others remain low relative to pre-pandemic levels. Brent crude oil prices were 31.0% lower in the third quarter of 2020 (y-o-y). The revised full-year forecast for 2020 projects oil prices to drop by 32.9% compared with the 42.6% initially forecast. The duration and severity of the pandemic pose the greatest risk to the forecast. On the other hand, prices of agricultural commodities have recovered from the declines earlier in the year, with the price index growing by 6.3% in the third quarter of 2020 (y-o-y). Lower production of some edible oils and meals, strong demand for raw materials, and a weaker United States dollar were the main drivers of the recovery. Latest full-year 2020 forecasts indicate a 2.8% growth in agricultural prices instead of a decline, and steady growth thereafter.

- The average price of liquefied natural gas fell by 34.3% in the third quarter of 2020 (y-o-y). Weaker demand for natural gas has been attributable to the COVID-19 pandemic and subsequent associated global recession, although the impact has been much smaller than for oil. The price is projected to decline by 17.9% for 2020 as a whole and to continue falling over the next few years. Cocoa prices have been broadly stable in the third quarter and are expected to grow modestly by 3.0% in 2020 as global demand picks up, following the slump during the lockdown. Meanwhile, the average price of Arabica coffee was up by 22.0% in the third quarter of 2020, with growth of 17.0% forecast for the full year. Gold prices continue to advance, rising by 29.6% in the third quarter of 2020 because of production disruptions and reduced gold recycling. These are seen to increase by 28.1% for the full year.

Tourism to the Pacific remains closed, recovery time frame uncertain

- As the pause in global tourism persists, Pacific destinations continue to receive minimal numbers of international travelers. In April–September 2020, monthly tourist arrivals in the Pacific declined by 99%–100% (y-o-y). Prospects for recovery remain highly uncertain, with plans for potential travel bubbles and other similar arrangements stalled by lingering health safety issues. In the North Pacific, a planned travel bubble between Palau and Taipei,China was postponed in late October because of Palau's concerns regarding its health system's capacity to manage potential COVID-19 cases or outbreaks. Further, although the first stage of the trans-Tasman travel bubble was opened in mid-October— allowing one-way travel without quarantine from New Zealand to select destinations in Australia (i.e., Australian Capital Territory, New South Wales, and Northern Territory)—full implementation was delayed in view of a second wave of COVID-19 cases in Victoria. Thus, any expansion of this travel bubble to include South Pacific destinations—perhaps starting with the Cook Islands, Fiji, and Niue—is likely to be pushed back into 2021 at the earliest.

COUNTRY ECONOMIC ISSUES

Cook Islands: a balancing act for economic recovery

Lead author: Lily Anne Homasi

The Cook Islands' tourism-dependent economy continues to be severely affected as the COVID-19 pandemic resulted in border closures that halted arrivals of visitors. With the shutdown of international travel, GDP is estimated to have declined by 7.0% for fiscal year (FY) 2020 (ended 30 June 2020) (Figure 1). Even if borders were to open in January 2021, the Asian Development Bank (ADB) anticipates that GDP would decline by 15.4% for FY2021. The contraction is expected to impact employment and household incomes, particularly for women who hold 60.5% of tourism-related jobs.

Figure 1: Cook Islands Economic Losses—Gross Domestic Product and Visitor Arrivals (year-on-year % change)

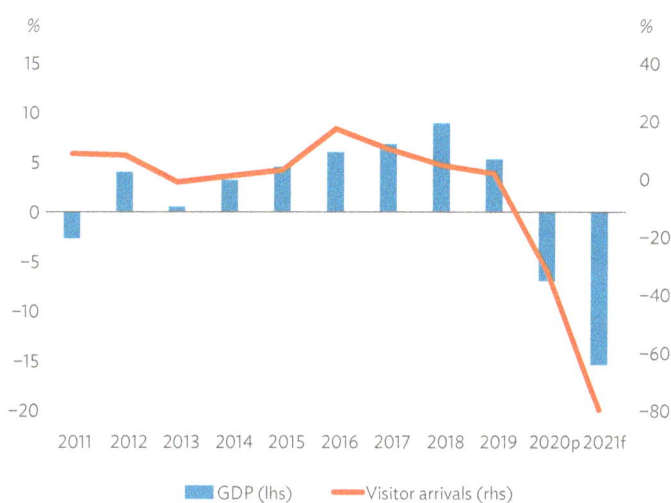

f = forecast, GDP = gross domestic product, lhs = left-hand scale,
p = preliminary, rhs = right-hand scale.
Note: Figures are based on fiscal year ended 30 June.
Sources: Government of the Cook Islands, Ministry of Finance; and Asian Development Bank estimates.

Countercyclical measures quickly deployed to relieve livelihoods and businesses. Anticipating the adverse impact of COVID-19 on the economy and people, the government quickly mobilized countercyclical measures that are supported through the Economic Response Plan (ERP) phases I (NZ$61 million, or 12.3% of GDP in FY2020) and II (NZ$76 million, or 17.7% of GDP in FY2021). The ERP is geared toward mitigating risks that are associated with the impact of COVID-19 on livelihood and businesses. They support the health system; and provide employment support and tax and credit relief for businesses, free or subsidized training, and cash grants to poor and vulnerable households. The wage subsidy channeled through employers and/or businesses (to retain workers in employment) is, by far, the single largest expenditure under the ERP, estimated at 17.9% of spending under phase I and 38.2% of that under phase II. Most support under the ERP was scheduled to be rolled out from

April to December 2020. In November, the government extended the implementation of the plan up to the end of February 2021 on the understanding that a travel bubble with New Zealand is expected to begin operations in early 2021. As of 27 November 2020, the Cook Islands has no reported cases of COVID-19. The extension to the wage subsidy recognizes that the business community requires additional funds to get itself ready for a pickup in economic activity. Although the injection from the stimulus package (12.3% of GDP in FY2020) helped to keep jobs and support some economic activity, the establishment of the travel bubble and resumption of visitor arrivals will be key to economic recovery.

Fiscal performance for FY2020 better than anticipated. The Government of the Cook Islands' preliminary results for FY2020, released in October 2020, revealed that the fiscal deficit was NZ$11.9 million, or 2.4% of GDP, much lower than the government's initial estimate of 12.4% of GDP (Figure 2). This is largely because income tax receipts (NZ$15.9 million) were higher than expected, and operational and capital expenditures (NZ$27.6 million and NZ$11.1 million lower, respectively) were significantly lower than expected. It is unclear whether the increase was a direct result of the stimulus package, or because of tax recovered from delayed tax returns. The smaller deficit would have less of an impact on government cash reserves, allowing some room for the government to sustain COVID-19 expenses, while it secures additional financing externally to continue to stimulate the economy and actively pursue the proposed travel bubble with New Zealand.

Figure 2: Fiscal Balances of Cook Islands

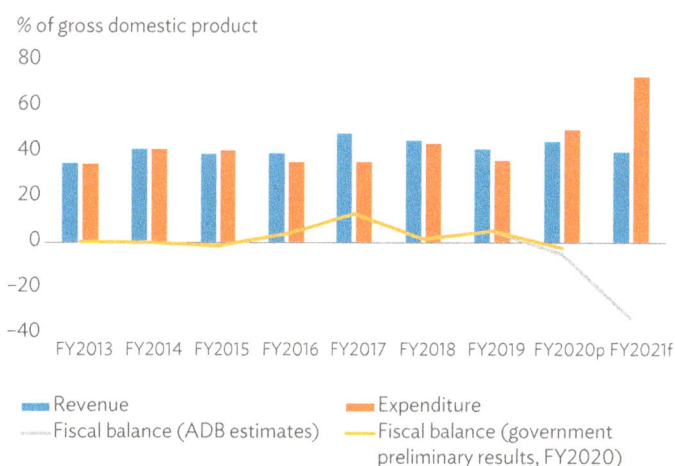

f = forecast, FY = fiscal year, p = preliminary.
Note: Figures are based on fiscal year ended 30 June.
Sources: Government of the Cook Islands, Ministry of Finance; and Asian Development Bank estimates.

A larger fiscal deficit in FY2021 and need for fiscal consolidation in the medium term. The ERP phase II is seen to contribute to a high budget deficit projected at 33.1% of GDP in FY2021, with the government anticipating cash reserves to be depleted as early as June 2021. Planned public sector management reforms are geared towards enhanced fiscal performance for a smooth recovery in the medium term. The crises in the mid-1990s and 2008–2009 helped the Government of the Cook Islands to enhance the resilience of its medium term fiscal management with the establishment and enforcement of target fiscal ratios. However, these ratios could benefit from a review, given that the impact of the COVID-19 pandemic is significantly larger than previous crises. The fiscal ratios and their thresholds should continue to be relevant and reflective of the medium term outlook that allows for short term fiscal expansion followed by medium term fiscal consolidation. For instance, increasing the debt-to-GDP threshold from the current ceiling of 35% of GDP to a reasonable threshold that provide this flexibility in the short term, but then adjust back to 35% in the medium term. The specific reforms—cash management, building fiscal buffers, enhanced monitoring of the ERP, strategic planning, and public financial management (PFM) targeted to improve domestic resource mobilization—should support overall improvements to the medium term fiscal framework in line with the government's draft economic development strategy.

More importantly, the Cook Islands is likely to be the first Pacific island country to launch a travel bubble with New Zealand. Discussions between the two countries are advanced, with the Government of New Zealand fielding a special mission to the Cook Islands from 14 November to consult with the government and other stakeholders on the readiness of the Cook Islands to safely open up and receive tourists. The findings from the mission are expected to inform areas to be strengthened before the bubble is launched. ADB is supporting the Government of the Cook Islands, including technical assistance to the Airport Authority Cook Islands to enhance the readiness of the Rarotonga International Airport. Coordinated efforts on this by stakeholders involved is key to ensuring a quick resumption of a safe travel zone that would help to revive the economy.

Additional financing would increase public debt in the near-term. Since closing the borders in March 2020, the government has been actively pursuing avenues to sustain the economy. Over FY2021–FY2022, government financing needs are estimated at $147.8 million. The government is expected to source this funding externally, mainly from the Government of New Zealand, ADB, and the Asian Infrastructure Investment Bank.[1] For many years, public net debt as a percentage of GDP[2] has been low—averaging 19.7% for the period FY2016–FY2019—and well within the government's threshold of 35.0%. With the fiscal expansion and additional borrowing, net public debt is expected to increase from 16.7% of GDP in FY2019 to 43.8% of GDP in FY2021. Although this will surpass the government's 35% threshold, ADB anticipates net debt to wind back and stay within its fiscal targets in FY2024 and onward.

Fiscal prudence and private sector investment key for sustainability. Fiscal policy is the key instrument for the government to steer development outcomes.[3] From FY2016 to FY2019, the fiscal surplus averaged 5.7%, following tax reforms in 2014. The fiscal surpluses allowed for the creation and buildup of fiscal buffers in the stabilization fund, which reached 11.4% of GDP in FY2020. The targeting of government spending on infrastructure would not only create jobs but also improve business environment through better services in information and communication technology, transport, electricity, and water and sewage. Such targeted spending would promote private sector investment in the economy, which in turn facilitates fiscal consolidation efforts. Having a medium-term fiscal strategy that considers quality public expenditures as well as fiscal sustainability would improve long-term economic outcomes.

Endnotes

[1]   The Cook Islands is not a member of the International Monetary Fund and the World Bank.

[2]   This is net of the Loan Reserve Fund, which averaged 0.9% of GDP during the same period.

[3]   The Cook Islands does not have a reserve bank and uses the New Zealand dollar as its currency; hence, there is no monetary policy.

References

Asian Development Bank (ADB). 2020a. *Asian Development Outlook. 2020: What Drives Innovation in Asia? Special Topic: The Impact of the Coronavirus Outbreak – An Update.* Manila.

ADB. 2020b. *Report and Recommendation of the President to the Board of Directors: Proposed Countercyclical Support Facility Loan to the Cook Islands for the COVID-19 Active Response and Economic Support Program.* Manila.

Government of the Cook Islands. 2020a. *Budget Estimates 2020/21.* Rarotonga. http://www.mfem.gov.ck/images/MFEM_Documents/Budget_Books/2020-21/2020 2024_Budget_Book_1_-_Estimates_-_Final.pdf.

Government of the Cook Islands. 2020b. *Financial Results for the year ending 30 June 2020.* Rarotonga.

Homasi, L. and J. Webb. 2020. Impacts of COVID-19 on the Cook Islands economy: Charting a path to recovery. *Pacific Economic Monitor.* July.

International Monetary Fund. 2020. Cook Islands Technical Assistance Report–Macroeconomic, Financial and Structural Policies. *IMF Country Report* No. 20/269. Washington, DC.

Fiji's long wait for tourism resumption

Lead author: Isoa Wainiqolo

The tourism-dependent Pacific island nation has won praises for its handling of the pandemic. It has been more than 7 months since the last case of community transmission and the government has declared the country "COVID-19 contained." However, the economic impact has been unprecedented, with no clear end in sight. Countercyclical fiscal and monetary policy measures have been implemented with the former constrained by the lack of fiscal space and the resultant increasing debt ratios. Monetary policy, on the other hand, benefitted from the strong foreign reserves position pre-crisis, aided by rising personal remittances. While the welfare of its populace should remain the priority of any government, fiscal policy needs to tread a fine line between providing additional stimulus to support recovery and keeping debt sustainability indicators in check.

To contain community transmission of COVID-19, the government implemented localized lockdowns, in consultation with the World Health Organization, while incoming passengers had to go through mandatory testing and 14 days quarantine in government monitored hotels. As of 7 December 2020, 35 out of the 42 confirmed cases had recovered, with 2 returning medical patients succumbing to the virus while in quarantine (Figure 3).

Figure 3: Confirmed COVID-19 Cases in Fiji

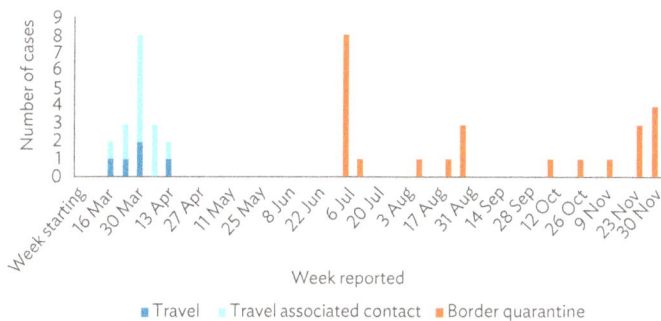

Source: Government of Fiji, Ministry of Health and Medical Services.

Despite the easing of restrictions, economic costs continue to mount. ADB projects the economy is likely to contract by 19.8% in 2020 and may only post a minimal recovery of 1.0% in 2021, assuming tourists start returning in the second half of the year.[1]

Recent indicators suggest significant declines in household demand. New consumption lending declined by 24.9% in the first nine months of 2021 while value-added tax collections declined by 41.2% attesting to low trading activity. On a positive note, remittances (4.9% of GDP in 2019) have held up, increasing 7.3% in the year to October. However, the contraction in GDP, stemming largely from declines in tourism, has had a profound impact on household incomes. Given the scale of the decline, the government decided to continue unemployment support for members of the

the Fiji National Provident Fund. As of 6 November, a total of F$136 million has been paid out to 177,000 members which includes F$43.7 million in government's contribution.[2]

The government announced its FY2021 (ends 31 July) budget on 17 July 2020, only 4 months after Parliament had passed an initial COVID-19 Response Budget. The impact of COVID-19 has been significant, with revenue as a percentage of GDP falling from 27.3% in FY2019 by 0.9 percentage points (pp) in FY2020 and a further 9.5 pp projected for FY2021 (Figure 4). Compared with FY2020, total revenue in FY2021 is expected to be 33.3% lower (with value-added tax collections down by 8.2% and custom duties down by 44.2%), while expenditure is projected to increase by 3.9%. The fiscal deficit is expected to increase to the equivalent of 20.2% of GDP in FY2021 from 8.2% in FY2020. Government debt is projected to increase from the equivalent of 49.3% of GDP at the end of FY2019 to 65.6% at the end of FY2020 and 83.4% the end of FY2021.

Figure 4: Fiji Fiscal Impact of COVID-19

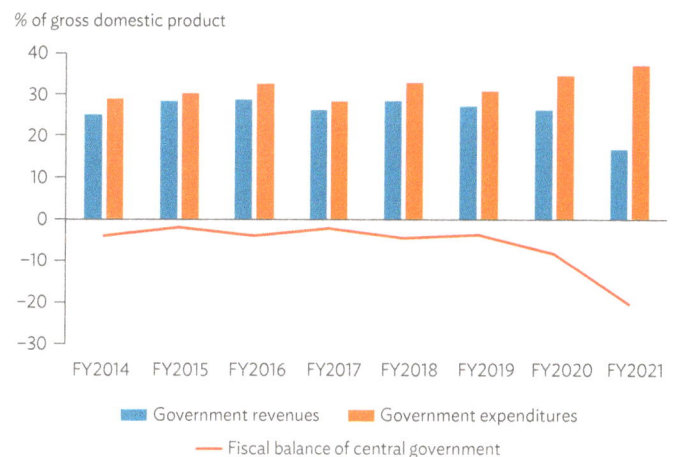

FY = fiscal year.
Note: From 2016, fiscal years end in July 31. Before 2016, fiscal years were based on calendar years. The FY2021 impact on revenue includes the lost revenue arising from the tax reductions undertaken by the Government of Fiji to revive the economy.
Source: Government of Fiji, budget documents.

The FY2021 budget reflects hopes of a travel bubble with the major tourist source markets of Australia and New Zealand before the end of 2020. Many of the new budget measures were specifically aimed at increasing tourism competitiveness when borders reopened. A F$400/tourist travel subsidy was allocated to the first 150,000 tourists to encourage forward bookings and support a quick recovery. The government also introduced a Blue Lane initiative[3] targeting yachts to dock in Fiji. Other measures aimed to simplify the tax system, reduce business operating costs by removing the service turnover tax, and ease the barriers to trade. Due to the extended border closures, most of these initiatives have so far had limited impact.

This creates a challenging environment for the government. Fiscal stimulus is still required to support business and household incomes, but some measures may need to be unwound earlier than anticipated to ensure fiscal sustainability. Normal revenue recovery from economic growth may not be enough to support ongoing spending needs, particularly if the recent reductions in effective tax rates are not compensated with new revenue sources. In the immediate term, there is an ongoing need for fiscal support, but in the medium term, fiscal consolidation will be an important policy agenda, for example by revisiting the revenue policies and improving expenditure targeting.

It is encouraging that the Fiji Revenue and Customs Service is continuing automation of processes by rolling out a new tax information system. This is likely to further lower compliance costs for taxpayers and provide real time data for better decision-making, forecasting, and planning to mitigate the likely revenue gap during the economic recovery.

Given the fall in revenues and the need for continued stimulus, the Government of Fiji increased its external borrowings. In the FY2021 budget, 51% of gross financing is expected to be financed by external loans, much larger than in previous years. The government optimized the financing mix considering the likely impact of the pandemic on local institutions, the low foreign interest rate environment, the increased commitment of multilateral partners and the loss of foreign currency earnings from tourism.

Liquidity has also improved with the central bank noting historical levels of bank demand deposits in August after drawdown of external loans. This has resulted in low interest rates which may result in improved lending activity during the recovery phase. However, in its latest Financial Stability Review, the central bank has indicated an increasing trend of nonperforming loans over the last 5 years.[4] Given the uncertainty surrounding the duration of the crisis, this may necessitate increased policy support until income levels normalize.

In the long term, the threat of climate change remains a major risk for fiscal management. Fiscal consolidation is key in creating the needed fiscal buffers to address any emerging shocks from natural hazards. Other external shocks, such as rise in oil prices, will also deteriorate the balance of payments position.

The government has been flexible in extending its support where it sees need. A cash-for-work program will be piloted in the western part of Fiji targeting informal workers—workers who would have been hit hard by the significant scaling down of that region's tourism industry. Full recovery of tourism and the economy will require the availability and distribution of the COVID-19 vaccine. Until then, a collective effort is required from all stakeholders in Fiji to minimize the economic impacts of border closures.

Endnotes

[1] The Government of Fiji released new calendar year growth projections on 24 November 2020. The economy is now forecast to contract by 19.0% in 2020 (compared with government forecast of -21.7% from July 2020), due to the agriculture sector performing better than anticipated, while contractions in the wholesale and retail trade, manufacturing, and construction sectors were lower than expected. The forecast of a recovery in 2021 was downgraded to a range between 1.6% and 8.0% (compared with government forecast of 14.1% in July 2020), due to revised assumptions on the speed of the recovery of the tourism sector. The current account deficit is now expected to deteriorate to -15.7% of GDP (compared with government forecast of -4.8% of GDP in July 2020).

[2] Affected employees draw down part of their superannuation funds (general balance) first. The government will top up those who do not have sufficient general account balance. By construction, 30% of superannuation contributions are in a general account with possible withdrawals for life-cycle events, while the rest is kept in a preserved account specifically for retirement purposes.

[3] It was an initiative targeting yachts who were looking for ports (given most Pacific island countries do not want to allow them in). So, if they have been out for more than 14 days since the last dock, then they are given a chance to berth provided their passengers and crew show negative COVID-19 test results.

[4] In its latest Financial Stability Review published in October 2019, the Reserve Bank of Fiji says that, despite an increasing trend over the last 5 years, nonperforming loans (NPLs) have "… remained at manageable level as majority of the households' NPLs are for housing loan which is understood to be adequately secured by properties." The central bank had also conducted stress tests as a check on the strength of Fiji's financial system and concluded that it can withstand a range of financial shocks.

References

Government of Fiji Ministry of Economy. 2020. *Economic and Fiscal Update Supplement to the 2020-2021 Budget Address.* Suva.

Government of Fiji Ministry of Economy. 2020. *Economic and Fiscal Update Supplement to the COVID-19 Response Budget Address.* Suva.

Government of Fiji Ministry of Health and Medical Services. 2020. *COVID-19 Update: 20th November 2020.* http://www.health.gov.fj/wp-content/uploads/2020/11/November-20th-Updates.pdf

Leaving no one behind: a look at the plight of the vulnerable in Kiribati and Tuvalu amid COVID-19

Lead authors: Noel Del Castillo, Lily Anne Homasi, and Isoa Wainiqolo

Like many other Pacific countries, prompt travel restrictions have ensured that Kiribati and Tuvalu are two of the few countries in the world that remain free from COVID-19 infection. The potential impact of a virus outbreak in both Kiribati and Tuvalu could be catastrophic because of the general living conditions of the population, weak national health systems, and complications arising from existing public health issues in both communicable and noncommunicable diseases.

Compared with other Pacific developing member countries, the economic impacts of COVID-19 are relatively limited in Kiribati and Tuvalu (Figure 1, page 33). Tourism industries in both countries are relatively small, so job losses in the sector will be minor in comparison with the total labor force. However, with the public sector already employing a large share of the workforce, it will not be able to absorb private sector workers who lose their jobs because of business closures. Outside of public sector employment, there are few alternative private sector jobs that are available for displaced workers. Any job losses will disproportionately affect the poor and vulnerable groups because social protection programs in these countries are relatively weak. Poor households and vulnerable groups will therefore require more attention and assistance for them to overcome the COVID-19 pandemic's impacts on household incomes.

Both countries have limited social protection for certain vulnerable groups: Kiribati has a senior citizen's benefit, disability support allowance, and the Copra Price Scheme;[1] Tuvalu has the Senior Citizen Scheme, a noncontributory old age pension, and the Disability Support Scheme. Both countries have provident funds—the Kiribati Provident Fund and the Tuvalu National Provident Fund (TNPF)—but these cover formal employees only.[2] In the face of an economic crisis, workers in the informal sector shoulder the brunt of the impacts in the absence of established programs that could provide financial protection and support.

KIRIBATI

When the Government of Kiribati declared a State of Public Emergency on 26 March, it closed ports of entry to the country, imposed closures of businesses and schools, prohibited community gatherings, and embarked on public health awareness campaigns to enforce physical distancing and hygiene practices. Reduced economic activity resulted in forgone earnings for businesses and job losses for workers.

Almost 280 workers have already been laid off, and many businesses are still considering reducing employment or available hours (ADB 2020a). The Government of Kiribati estimates that 1,040 people (3.7% of the Kiribati working population of 28,158) have been affected, with 69% working in the domestic market and 31% working overseas. Containment measures in other countries, particularly in Kiribati's major import partners (Australia and Fiji), have also resulted in reduced supply because of the closure of nonessential services, longer manufacturing times because of reduced workforce, and logistics bottlenecks in the shipping of basic food items and construction materials. It created an atmosphere of panic buying, which adversely affected the poor and the vulnerable who are incapable of buying in bulk. Since March 2020, supply of essential foods has improved with container ships arriving in the country every month.

The pandemic has been problematic particularly for the travel industry. The tourism sector lost almost A\$1 million in forgone revenue and laid off 159 workers (ADB 2020a). Three locally based international travel agencies have now closed and about 20 employees were laid off. Domestic air travel has been erratic because of the inability to source spare parts on time. Many I-Kiribati were stranded in foreign ports as governments implemented their containment measures. Those stranded included government employees on official travel, students, and overseas workers whose contracts have expired. There are 30 seafarers working on South Pacific Marine Services vessels that are stranded in Fiji and Australia, and 26 temporary contract workers in Australia that have been laid off and are unable to return home.

Most of the impacts discussed above pertain to employment in the formal sector. However, the impact of the pandemic on the workers in the informal sector is more severe in the absence of social security benefits that formal sector workers have access to. An ADB rapid assessment estimates that the informal sector in Kiribati is equivalent to 40% of the country's labor force. About 400 individuals lost their sources of livelihood, mostly coming from the informal sector. This does not include workers in construction and other trade industries, engaged by private contractors on job availability—usually offered by the government in executing large development projects, such as the South Tarawa Water Supply and the Outer Islands Road projects. These projects were supposed to start in 2020, but have been pushed back because of the pandemic delaying the transportation of critical staff from overseas. Many in urban areas have been deprived of income, such as those working in small private businesses, roadside vendors, and fisherfolk.

To mitigate the impacts of the pandemic, the government mobilized a National COVID-19 Preparedness and Response Plan.[3] This provided A\$11.7 million for health preparedness measures, A\$3.2 million for social protection programs, and A\$0.8 million for support to overseas workers and students. Almost three-quarters of the allocation to social protection programs are channeled to assist workers who have lost their jobs (Figure 5). The government initiated a cash grant of A\$360 per month across the board from June to August 2020. This support covers both resident and nonresident formal-sector workers whose employment has been terminated, suspended, or reduced. The response plan also provided support to stranded I-Kiribati workers overseas by subsidizing their accommodation and daily subsistence costs incurred by the employers. The social assistance programs of the government came in the form of financial support to students and other citizens stranded overseas.

However, a closer look at these programs indicates that they cater only to workers in the formal sector. To avail of the unemployment income support program, applicants must be a member of the Kiribati Provident Fund, while the private sector employers must be active members of the Kiribati Chamber of Commerce & Industry. Those who belong to the informal sector are not members of the Kiribati Provident Fund, and many of their employers are not members of the Kiribati Chamber of Commerce & Industry. Vulnerable groups, who depend on the income of workers in the informal sector, are at a disadvantage when informal sector workers are excluded from these programs. And while the government has allocated A$72.6 million for social protection programs (support to older persons and the unemployed) in its 2020 national budget, limited data on the vulnerable can prevent these programs from reaching them.

Another important component of the government's response plan is the communication and awareness component, and the importance of ensuring that everyone has access to information. However, the communication strategies heavily rely on traditional mass media delivery mechanisms (mainly radio and newspaper) without taking into account that just over 40% of households have access to a radio—the primary source of information (ADB 2020a). The remaining 60% rely on word of mouth for information.

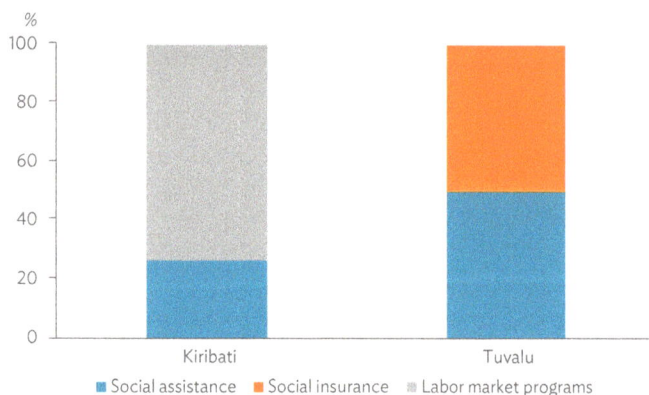

Figure 5: Social Protection Measures
in the COVID-19 Response Plans of Kiribati and Tuvalu

COVID-19 = coronavirus disease.
Sources: ADB estimates using data from COVID-19 response packages and fiscal budget documents of Kiribati and Tuvalu.

TUVALU

The Government of Tuvalu's declaration of a State of Emergency on 20 March was followed by the closure of its ports of entry, prohibition of public gatherings, and temporary school shutdown—all aimed at preventing the entry and spread of COVID-19. The government approved its COVID-19 prevention plan in March 2020, even before Fiji (main entry point to Tuvalu) recorded its first case on 18 March. A taskforce was created as soon as the imminent threat of the pandemic was identified. A supplementary budget was passed in March 2020, which included A$5.7 million for the procurement of personal protective equipment, ventilators, COVID-19 testing equipment, and other supplies.[4]

Global travel restrictions have seriously affected the tourism-related businesses, mainly composed of accommodation providers and handicraft producers. Out of the 40 employees in the tourism sector, 17 were made redundant. While the layoffs are regrettable, the restrictions put in place are necessary as the alternative would be an overwhelmed health system unable to meet the demands of the pandemic.

Prior to the pandemic, there were about 920 unemployed women residing in Funafuti, Tuvalu's capital (ADB 2020b). Some had started to become involved in handicraft businesses, relying heavily on international tourists and government visitors. Most of these are small and medium-sized enterprises. As the pandemic pushed the government to adopt containment and defensive measures, these businesses lost their only source of income. Hotels were also forced to lay off some of their employees, most of which are women, or reduce their working hours. With losses piling up, these businesses shifted their operations to other related ventures such as restaurants and cafés, but income is substantially smaller compared with what they used to earn before the pandemic.

Like many Pacific island countries, Tuvalu is highly dependent on imported basic commodities. As the government closed its international ports of entry, it initially fueled speculation that imported food items would no longer be able to enter the country. This created panic among consumers who rushed into shops and purchased basic commodities such as sugar, rice, flour, and biscuits in bulk. The spike in demand for these food items led to the skyrocketing of prices, to the disadvantage of those with meager incomes. It only abated after the government regulated the purchase of basic commodities by issuing food vouchers to all households. This ensured that everyone had equal access to the items and that supplies would last until the next cargo ship arrived.

The closure of schools disrupted learning, especially since the schools were not prepared to provide alternative means of delivering education at a distance. Some parents refused to allow their children to return to school when they reopened. Given the logistical constraints of interisland ferries, parents are concerned that their children might not be able to return home immediately should there be an outbreak of COVID-19 in the country. While the government continues to improve e-learning to make it a viable alternative to physical learning, it is expensive and cannot be availed of by those who have no regular income. Another challenge to e-learning is the unreliable internet connection in the country.

The government launched its *Talaaliki Plan* to prepare for a worst case scenario. Its proposed spending for social protection programs is almost evenly split between social assistance and social insurance (Figure 5). A huge part of the government's social assistance program came in the form of a universal cash transfer of A$40 per person, which was paid out in April and May, providing immediate economic relief for all in the country. Meanwhile, the government's social insurance program was carried out through the TNPF. It introduced a one-time COVID-19 payout benefit of A$500 for its members and a 3-month cash benefit payout support for workers who have been terminated or are working with a reduced wage. TNPF also offered loan restructuring and suspension of loan repayments.

The universal cash transfer program was met both with praise and criticism. It provided temporary income support to many informal workers who are not members of the TNPF. At the same time, however, critics pointed out that the A\$40 cash transfer per person is inadequate to sustain the needs of every individual. The 2-month payout was provided to all Tuvaluans, including those who are receiving a monthly pension and even the more affluent individuals. The government decided to limit beneficiaries to people without regular incomes only in June. A more targeted payment specifically for vulnerable groups would have allowed for increased adequacy within the existing fiscal envelope.

Concluding remarks

Government provision of immediate economic relief is a step in the right direction, which becomes more important in an environment of weak social protection systems. Job and income losses are not spread equally, and those impacted have few other options to turn to in terms of public support. Basic social protection programs that are already in place could be further expanded and strengthened, particularly the system that helps to facilitate superannuation and unemployment payments in a timely manner. Such reform could be supported by technical assistance grants from development partners. In the face of any crisis, such as this pandemic, effective response plans must ensure that the needs of poor and the vulnerable groups are properly accounted for. In countries like Kiribati and Tuvalu, geographical remoteness and isolation create an additional hurdle to effective government response. It has limited information on where affected people are, how to assess their relative need, and how best to distribute aid.

The governments of Kiribati and Tuvalu can further improve their response packages and address fiscal sustainability issues surrounding social protection spending through better-targeted programs and, in the long term, broader and effective social protection coverage.

Endnotes

[1]   A subsidy which effectively serves as a large cash transfer for outer islands households.

[2]   Formal sector refers to employment in the public sector, including state-owned enterprises, and registered companies/businesses. The informal sector involves the people employed as casual labor, people in the villages, and those who run small business enterprises that are not formally registered with government.

[3]   For additional details on the broad impact of the pandemic and response of the Government of Kiribati, please refer to Homasi and Wainiqolo, 2020.

[4]   For additional details on the broad impact of the pandemic and response of the Government of Tuvalu, please refer to Homasi and Wainiqolo, 2020.

References

Asian Development Bank (ADB). 2020a. COVID-19 Rapid Assessment Report–Kiribati. Unpublished.

ADB. 2020b. Rapid Assessment Report 2020–Tuvalu. Unpublished.

Government of Kiribati. 2020a. *National COVID-19 Preparedness and Response Plan*. Tarawa.

Government of Kiribati. 2020b. *National Budget.* Tarawa.

Government of Tuvalu. 2020. *National COVID-19 Taskforce Talaaliki Plan*. Funafuti.

Homasi, L. and I. Wainiqolo. 2020. Impacts of COVID-19 on small economies–Kiribati and Tuvalu: Recasting essential reforms. *Pacific Economic Monitor.* July.

Addressing the economic challenges of COVID-19 in the Federated States of Micronesia and the Marshall Islands

Lead authors: Cara Tinio and Rommel Rabanal

The previous issue of the *Pacific Economic Monitor* explored the near-term economic outlook of the Federated States of Micronesia (FSM) and the Marshall Islands amid the COVID-19 pandemic. Further information, coupled with expectations that border closures and travel restrictions will run well into 2021, now suggests that the negative socioeconomic impacts on these economies would be more severe than initially estimated.

In both countries, the private sector is seen to experience the downturn more keenly than the public sector. Further, up to 70% of pandemic-related job losses in the FSM by the end of FY2021 (ends 30 September 2021 for both economies), and about a third of that those in the Marshall Islands, are estimated to affect women. Informal workers and small, cash-based businesses are also particularly vulnerable. The resulting losses in income will make it more difficult for households to afford their basic needs, exacerbated by shipping delays because of travel and quarantine restrictions that limit the supply of imported food and other essential commodities. ADB predicts that, by the end of FY2021, the poverty rate will rise to more than 36% of the population in the FSM, and more than one-third of the population in the Marshall Islands. Increased poverty and hardship will contribute to declines in social cohesion, including higher risk of gender-based violence (GBV). Further, prolonged local mobility restrictions will disrupt access to education and health care, affecting human capital development and long-term prospects for growth.

In response to these challenges, the governments of the FSM and the Marshall Islands have developed plans to strengthen their respective health-care systems to prepare for, and manage, any local cases of COVID-19; temporarily assist businesses and workers affected by the pandemic; and reduce the vulnerabilities of the poor, older people, persons with disabilities, and women and girls. This article will examine efforts in the FSM and the Marshall Islands to build economic resilience to the COVID-19 pandemic.

FEDERATED STATES OF MICRONESIA

In addition to a $29.0 million COVID-19 Health Action Plan, the FSM government's countercyclical response program, to be implemented in FY2020–FY2021, includes an $18.4 million economic stimulus package (Figure 6). This package comprises: (i) the Tourism Mitigation Fund, which provides wage subsidies, social security payment and gross revenue tax rebates, and interest payment relief on business loans to qualified tourism businesses—as well as those in other sectors, subject to approval by Congress—and temporary unemployment assistance to migrant workers who have lost their jobs because of the pandemic; and (ii) concessional lending, through the FSM Development Bank, of up to $10,000 to microenterprises and up to $30,000 to small enterprises. In addition to the government's economic stimulus package, citizens of the FSM and the United States (US) who have lost their jobs or must work fewer hours because of the pandemic are receiving temporary unemployment assistance under the US Coronavirus Aid, Relief, and Economic Security Act of 2020.

The FSM program also includes social protection programs totaling $11.3 million. These cover the following:

- a one-time $500 cash transfer to eligible low-income households, with additional benefits for those that are headed by a woman or include persons with disability or dependent older persons and children (the amount for this component will total $5 million);

- a food security program for community groups and low-income households, which will provide subsistence livelihood training and distribute seeds and planting and fishing materials, as well as deliver food rations in the event of any COVID-19 cases in the country ($2 million);

- small grants to civil society organizations for increasing COVID-19 awareness and preparedness, and GBV prevention, in communities ($2 million); and

- other assistance to vulnerable groups, including temporary waivers of medical expenses for older people, persons with disability, and GBV survivors; electricity subsidies and solar lamps for off-grid households in outer islands; increased community health center support for GBV survivors; and one-off cash payments to FSM citizens and students stranded abroad ($2.3 million in total).

MARSHALL ISLANDS

The Republic of the Marshall Islands Coronavirus Preparedness and Response Plan, approved in June 2020, outlines the actions and resources required to (i) strengthen the health system's capacity for enhanced surveillance, infection control, and case management, particularly in Majuro and Ebeye, the country's largest population centers and main points of entry ($21.1 million); (ii) provide economic relief and recovery assistance to businesses adversely affected by prevailing travel restrictions ($12.4 million); (iii) safeguard the well-being of vulnerable communities and households, including those in the more remote parts of the Marshall Islands ($8.3 million); and (iv) ensure the continuity of essential services, including utilities, and support consular assistance and possible evacuation of citizens abroad ($4.0 million) (Figure 7). The plan will be implemented in FY2020–FY2021.

Figure 6: Federated States of Micronesia Countercyclical Response Program

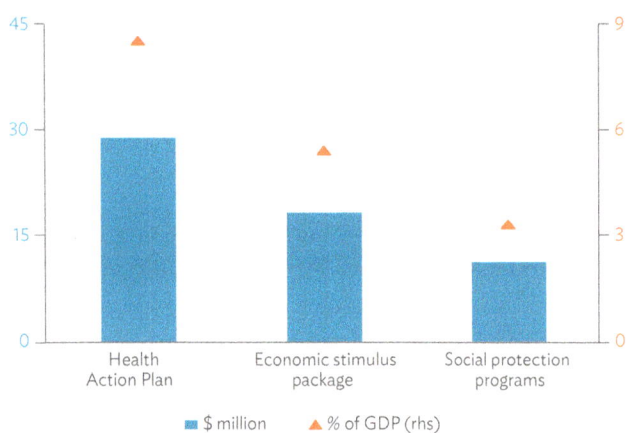

GDP = gross domestic product, rhs = right-hand scale.
Source: Asian Development Bank. 2020. *Report and Recommendation of the President to the Board of Directors: Proposed Countercyclical Support Facility Grant to the Federated States of Micronesia for the Health Expenditure and Livelihoods Support Program*. Manila.

Figure 7: Republic of the Marshall Islands Coronavirus Preparedness and Response Plan

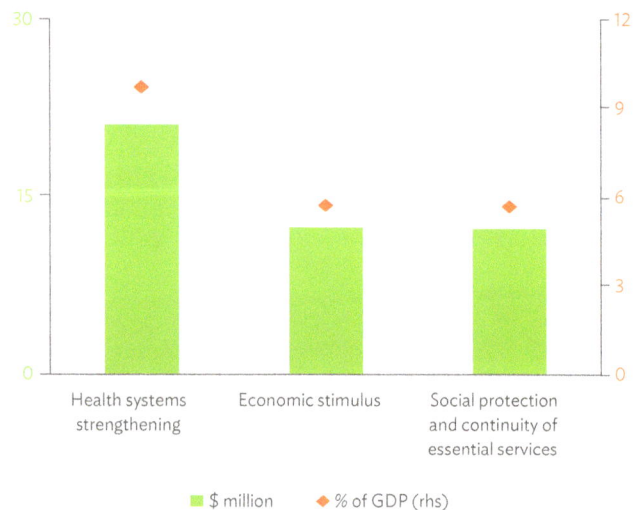

GDP = gross domestic product, rhs = right-hand scale.
Source: Asian Development Bank. 2020. *Report and Recommendation of the President to the Board of Directors: Proposed Countercyclical Support Facility Grant to the Republic of the Marshall Islands for the Health Expenditure and Livelihoods Support Program*. Manila.

The economic assistance component provides $900–$50,000 in assistance to tourism-related businesses affected by the travel restrictions, as well as to eligible enterprises that can show proof, based on their tax filings, of adverse impacts from the COVID-19 pandemic. Small and informal businesses can also qualify for assistance, though they would receive the minimum payment in the absence of supporting documentation. This component will also support the local production of fabric facemasks, hospital gowns and beddings, and virgin coconut oil that will mostly benefit women and informal workers. Finally, it seeks to assist business owners in managing their costs, perhaps via utilities discounts or guaranteed or low-interest loans, and safely resuming operations by helping to fund protective equipment and transport arrangements (in line with social distancing protocols) for their workers.

Assistance to the vulnerable involves providing monthly food baskets (comprising shelf-stable staples, e.g., rice, flour, and sugar) to each household in the more remote islands and atolls for at least 6 months, as well as fishing gear and farming tools. Further, the plan expands the Ministry of Education's feeding program, which now provides school lunch meals 5 days a week to about 11,300 children from poor families nationwide. This component will also help expand water, sanitation, and hygiene facilities, implement gender-sensitive protocols in quarantine shelters, and support continuing children's education.

The Marshall Islands also receives temporary unemployment assistance from the US under the Coronavirus Aid, Relief, and Economic Security Act of 2020, and is working to sustain ongoing, pre-pandemic social protection programs specifically targeting vulnerable groups. Among others, these include a special education program for disabled children aged 3–21, training programs for youth with little formal education or who cannot continue secondary education, free maternal and reproductive health services, and the national social insurance scheme.

Keeping the lights on while awaiting the "new normal"

Both the FSM and the Marshall Islands are working to fuel their economies through the crisis brought about by the pandemic. Assistance to affected businesses, whether in the form of direct cash infusions or measures to reduce costs, would help them stay operational and retain their workers. The support targeted to micro and small enterprises and informal businesses would help them adapt to challenging conditions and even capitalize on any opportunities that may arise (e.g., increased demand for face masks). The Marshall Islands' plan can also enable businesses to safeguard their employees' health and safety amid increased concerns brought about by the pandemic. These could have spillover effects to related sectors in the FSM and the Marshall Islands economies from which beneficiary businesses would source the goods and services used in their operations.

Meanwhile, cash payments such as those under the FSM economic stimulus package and social protection programs will help bolster consumer demand, especially among low-income households facing tighter financial circumstances, as well as the wholesale/retail trade sectors. Cash transfers to low-income households could also serve as support to informal workers affected by the pandemic. It must also be noted that the health-related components of the FSM and the Marshall Islands plans, in building COVID-19 preparedness and response, are helping to minimize the chances of a local outbreak that will require tighter local mobility restrictions and further hamper domestic demand. (Although, as of this writing, four arrivals to Kwajalein Atoll have tested positive for COVID-19, all were under quarantine at the border following set protocols and no risk of community transmission has been identified.) Efforts to sustain education and provide livelihood training would help the youth and vulnerable communities to develop knowledge and practical skills that should benefit them in the future.

Although the expenditures necessitated by the COVID-19 response plans are estimated to have significantly increased the financing needs of both the governments of the FSM and the Marshall Islands in FY2020–FY2021, these are not expected to cause a corresponding increase in public borrowing. Grant assistance from development partners, along with governments' own funds from domestic resource mobilization and reprioritization of expenditures, will fully cover the FSM and the Marshall Islands plans. Household rapid vulnerability assessments supported by the International Organization for Migration are helping the Government of the Marshall Islands to calibrate and channel assistance to the most vulnerable households in Majuro and Ebeye, and ADB helped to develop the social protection components of the FSM's COVID-19 response.

Taken together, the various components of the respective COVID-19 response plans of the FSM and the Marshall Islands are expected to help position businesses and workers to benefit once border and travel restrictions are lifted. Efforts to safeguard public health, provide training and education, and protect the vulnerable will help the population to avoid the spread of disease and withstand the social impacts of the pandemic. These efforts will help the FSM and the Marshall Islands to weather the ongoing COVID-19 crisis, while laying the foundations for strong and sustainable economic recovery.

References

ADB. 2020. *Report and Recommendation of the President to the Board of Directors: Proposed Countercyclical Support Facility Grant to the Federated States of Micronesia for the Health Expenditure and Livelihoods Support Program*. Manila.

ADB. 2020. *Report and Recommendation of the President to the Board of Directors: Proposed Countercyclical Support Facility Grant to the Republic of the Marshall Islands for the Health Expenditure and Livelihoods Support Program*. Manila.

The Marshall Islands Journal. 2020. RMI's Covid-free status ends. 5 November.

The Marshall Islands Journal. 2020. Kwaj system did its job. 5 November.

Tinio, C. and R. Rabanal. 2020. Remoteness redux: COVID-19 impacts in the Federated States of Micronesia and the Marshall Islands. *Pacific Economic Monitor*. July.

Keeping Nauru's economy moving

Lead authors: Jacqueline Connell and Prince Cruz

Although COVID-19 has had a relatively mild impact on Nauru's economy, government spending on containment, health preparedness, and keeping state-owned enterprises (SOEs) afloat was equivalent to 7.8% of GDP in fiscal year (FY) 2020, ending 30 June 2020. The FY2021 budget, announced in June, continued the government's response to COVID-19, including through subsidizing air and sea freight services that were disrupted by COVID-19, but are critical for the nation's supply of food, fuel, and medical equipment. With more than half of the government's COVID-19 response expected to be channeled through SOEs, ongoing attention is needed on their performance and governance.

Nauru's public administration and SOEs are major generators of demand. Together, they employ almost two-thirds of the labor force. Their continued operation, together with the government's successful containment efforts, has lessened the impact of COVID-19 on jobs, and helped prevent a major economic downturn. Economic growth is estimated to have slowed slightly to 0.7% in FY2020 (from 1.0% in FY2019), making Nauru one of the few economies to avoid GDP contraction (IMF 2020).

The government's fiscal response to COVID-19 in FY2020 focused on containment measures, including provision of quarantine facilities for international arrivals; health preparedness (such as procurement of testing equipment and personal protective equipment, and upgrade of the only hospital); repatriation of Nauruans; a stimulus "ex gratia" payment to pensioners and public employees (including SOEs); and support to Nauru Airlines (Figure 8). State-owned Nauru Airlines, the sole airline servicing the country, faced a sharp decline in passenger traffic because of containment measures. International flights were reduced to once every 2 weeks, and quarantine was imposed on passenger arrivals. The fiscal response was coordinated by a COVID-19 Taskforce, established in March.

The FY2021 budget increased funding for the national airline to maintain regular air freight services. It also introduced funding for the state-owned port authority to charter a cargo ship to reduce reliance on the one shipping company that served Nauru (Government of Nauru 2020b).

With SOEs involved in a range of commercial and noncommercial activities, contributing about half of GDP, their performance has a profound effect on the people of Nauru. High operating costs—typical in small island economies—combined with low tariffs or directives to deliver noncommercial objectives have forced some SOEs to rely on large subsidies, posing a risk to fiscal sustainability.

Subsidies to SOEs increased significantly in FY2020, rising to the equivalent of 21.0% of GDP (Figure 9). These subsidies were more than the government spent on health, education, and police combined, indicating the significant social and economic cost of subsidizing SOEs. Dividends to the government, as owner of the SOEs, amounted to only 1.3% of GDP in FY2020 and were less in the previous 2 years.

Figure 8: Nauru COVID-19 Spending

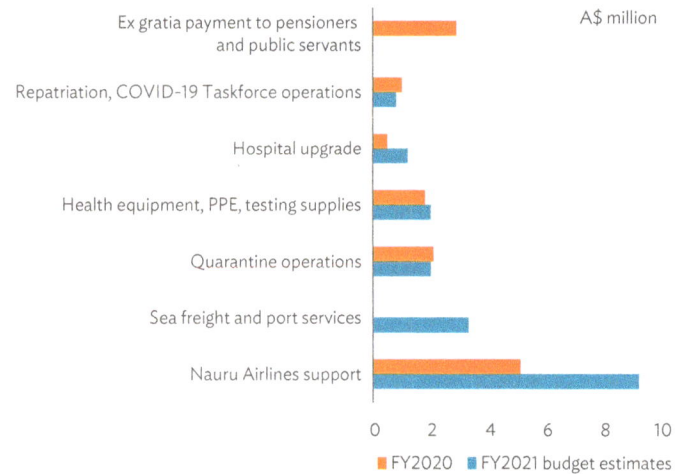

COVID-19 = coronavirus disease, FY = fiscal year, PPE = personal protective equipment.
Source: ADB estimates based on Government of Nauru. 2020. *2019–20 Final Budget Outcome*. Yaren; and Government of Nauru. 2020. *2020–21 Budget and Estimates of Revenue and Expenditure, Budget Paper No. 1, Budget Strategy and Outlook*. Yaren.

Figure 9: Government of Nauru Expenditure

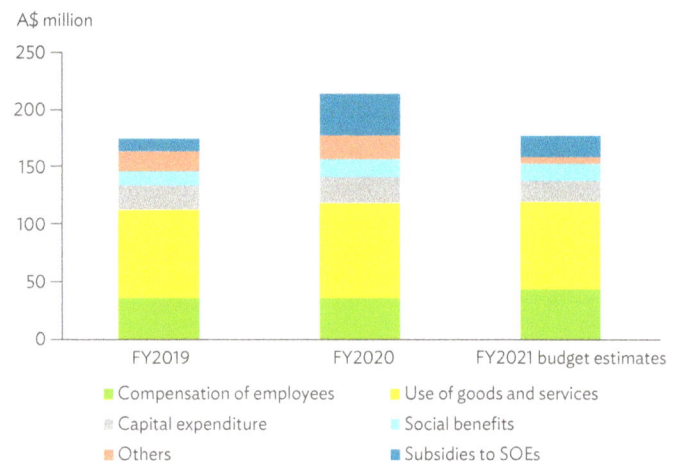

FY = fiscal year, SOE = state-owned enterprise.
Source: Asian Development Bank estimates based on Government of Nauru. 2020. *2019–20 Final Budget Outcome*. Yaren; Government of Nauru. 2020. *2020–21 Budget and Estimates of Revenue and Expenditure, Budget Paper No. 1, Budget Strategy and Outlook*. Yaren; and Government of Nauru. 2019. *Budget and Estimates of Revenue and Expenditure, Budget Paper No. 1, Budget Strategy and Outlook*. Yaren.

SOE reform to promote fiscal sustainability should ensure the continued provision of essential services, whether by the private or public sector, while minimizing the government's fiscal burden. In June 2019, the Public Enterprise Act, establishing a legislative framework for SOEs to be commercially successful. The act recognizes that some SOEs are directed to pursue noncommercial objectives, and establishes processes to ensure that the delivery of community service obligations does not compromise the efficient operation of SOEs.

With fishing license fees, taxation, and revenues related to the Regional Processing Centre for asylum seekers remaining strong in FY2020, the government had the fiscal space to mitigate the economic, social, and supply-chain risks of COVID-19, and still deliver a sizeable fiscal surplus. The challenge ahead is to ensure that critical services are delivered efficiently, and that private sector activities are not adversely affected. Reducing the fiscal risks posed by some SOEs will be increasingly important if government revenues decline over the medium term because of falling revenue from fishing licenses or because the Regional Processing Centre is scaled down.

References

International Monetary Fund. 2020. *World Economic Outlook, October 2020: A Long and Difficult Ascent.* Washington, DC.

Government of Nauru. 2020a. *2019–2020 Final Budget Outcome.* Yaren.

Government of Nauru. 2020b. *2020–21 Budget and Estimates of Revenue and Expenditure, Budget Paper No. 1, Budget Strategy and Outlook.* Yaren.

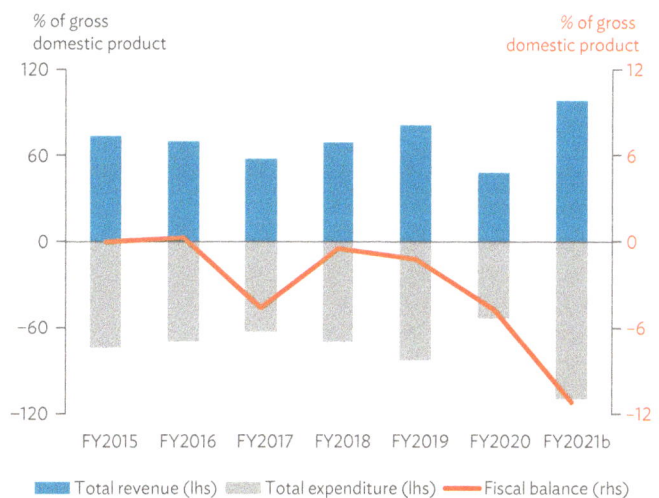

Figure 10: Niue Fiscal Accounts, FY2015–FY2021

b = budgeted, FY = fiscal year, lhs = left-hand scale, rhs = right-hand scale.
Sources: Government of Niue. 2020. *Estimates of Expenditure and Revenue for Financial Year 2020/2021.* Alofi; and Asian Development Bank estimates.

Niue: A travel bubble to lift fiscal pressures?

Lead author: Rommel Rabanal

Beyond the well-documented impacts on Niue's vital tourism sector, data from the FY2021 (ends 20 June 2021) budget provide further context of the COVID-19 pandemic's impacts. Outturns for FY2020 show that revenue fell by 4.2% largely because of subdued economic activity with no tourism since late March 2020. Further, implementation of development partner-financed capital projects was stalled during the year, partly because of prevailing travel disruptions. Combined, these factors imply that a severe economic contraction occurred during FY2020. With a 4.1% increase in recurrent spending to prepare for, and respond to, COVID-19 impacts, the fiscal deficit widened to the equivalent of 4.7% of GDP in FY2020 from 1.2% the previous year.

Further, while previous budgets have usually targeted at least maintaining fiscal balance, the budget for FY2021 projects a further widening of the deficit to the equivalent of 11.2% of GDP (Figure 10). This is mostly because of a 21.2% increase in recurrent spending to sustain COVID-19 impact mitigation measures, principally for continuing operations of the Niue Power Corporation amid deferred payments from consumers. With support from New Zealand, the FY2021 budget also includes continuing COVID-19 assistance measures for health (equivalent to 1.5% of GDP), food security (0.8%), and private sector relief (3.3%), among others. This would be comparable with the 15.5% increase recorded in FY2018 when the economy grew strongly.

On the revenue side, the FY2021 budget targets a 14.0% expansion from the previous year.

During the last quarter of 2020, officials from health and border agencies of Niue and New Zealand have ramped up discussions on a potential travel bubble between the two countries. New Zealand, the World Health Organization, and the Pacific Community are all providing technical assistance to Niue to ensure that necessary systems are in place to support safe, quarantine-free travel. Establishing shared protocols for safeguarding public health that are acceptable to both parties will be a critical prerequisite for any resumption of international travel. Based on public statements in early November 2020, both the Premier of Niue and the Prime Minister of New Zealand appear confident that a travel bubble will be in place soon. Although such an arrangement would provide a welcome boost to Niue's tourism sector and the broader economy during the latter half of FY2021, this is unlikely to translate to gains in government revenue that will be enough to stave off the expected widening of the fiscal deficit. Nonetheless, the successful implementation of a travel bubble that avoids any COVID-19 outbreaks can lay the foundation for economic recovery and a return to fiscal sustainability.

Reference

Government of Niue. 2020. *Estimates of Expenditure and Revenue for Financial Year 2020/2021.* Alofi.

Palau: Reforms for sustainable recovery from the COVID-19 crisis

Lead author: Rommel Rabanal

The economy of Palau contracted by 13.8% in FY2020 (ended 30 September 2020). This is deeper than the earlier projection of a 9.5% decline in the July 2020 issue of the *Pacific Economic Monitor*—reflecting even stronger-than-expected adverse impacts of COVID-19 travel restrictions on business activity and household incomes. A further decline of 13.2% is seen for FY2021 (a downgrade from the previous projection of 12.8%) with tourism unlikely to restart during this fiscal year. Reduced business activity has constrained tax collections, which declined by about 25% in FY2020 and are set for a similar fall in FY2021. With additional spending of $20 million under the Coronavirus Relief One-Stop Shop Program to mitigate the pandemic's impacts on the private sector, a fiscal deficit equivalent to 13% of GDP was recorded in FY2020. Fiscal deficits equivalent to 24% of GDP in FY2021—in part reflecting additional spending of $12 million necessary to extend assistance measures until the end of the fiscal year—and a further 11% in FY2022 are projected over the near-term.

These deficits translate to total financing requirements of about $110 million during FY2020–FY2022, of which about $100 million will be met through new external borrowing and the balance by drawdowns from government deposits. This is seen to push Palau's debt-to-GDP ratio to a peak of close to 80% in FY2022 (Figure 11). However, assuming economic recovery commences with a reopening of tourism in FY2022, the debt-to-GDP ratio is projected to steadily decline to the pre-COVID-19 level of about 30% by FY2030, even under conservative long-run growth assumptions.

Figure 11: Palau Projected Public Debt

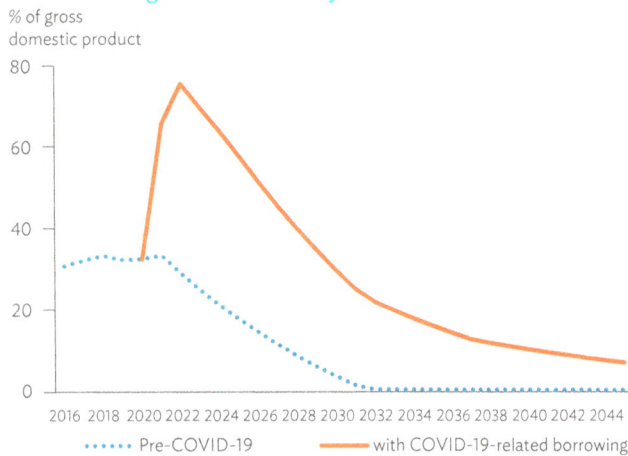

COVID-19 = coronavirus disease.
Source: Asian Development Bank estimates.

Nonetheless, with COVID-19 necessitating unprecedented levels of borrowing, it will be imperative for Palau to carve sufficient fiscal space to service its debt. Assuming new debt will be incurred under concessional terms, debt service requirements associated with COVID-19-related borrowing are estimated to reach about

$4.7 million per year after loan grace periods. On top of debt servicing of $8 million–$9 million per annum in the years leading up to the pandemic, debt service requirements are expected to increase to up to $14 million per year by FY2026–FY2027. Even if Palau's fiscal accounts can revert to pre-COVID-19 trends—where annual surpluses equivalent to 4.0% of GDP were recorded during FY2015–FY2019—by FY2023 and onward, available resources could fall short of debt servicing requirements in some years.

To avoid sudden cuts to expenditure, which can create fiscal space but likely at the expense of forgone stimulus to the economy, Palau can consider implementing revenue-raising reforms to tax policy along with a shift to a more growth-enhancing expenditure mix that prioritizes capital spending, among others. Palau's current tax system relies heavily on gross revenue taxes and import duties—together accounting for half of annual collections—that are inefficient, distortionary, and discourage private investment, particularly startups. During FY2015–FY2019, Palau's tax-to-GDP ratio was 20.2%, below the 24.4%–29.0% range for other tourism-dependent Pacific countries such as the Cook Islands, Fiji, and Samoa. Further, with user fees set below full cost recovery, the Palau Public Utilities Corporation has required subsidies averaging $1.5 million per annum (2.3% of recurrent spending) in FY2013–FY2016 and again in FY2019. Similarly, Palau's social security funds received transfers totaling $3.7 million (3.4% of recurrent spending) in FY2019, with needs seen to rise given substantial unfunded liabilities. Rising recurrent spending has translated to some offsetting reductions in capital spending in recent years.

A tax reform program that involves the introduction of a value-added tax can help boost Palau's tax-to-GDP ratio through collection efficiency gains. Simplified simulations show that, if tax reform can raise the tax-to-GDP ratio gradually by 0.25 percentage points per year from FY2024—such that it increases by a full percentage point by FY2027 and onwards—the higher debt service requirements stemming from COVID-19-related borrowing can largely be covered (Figure 12). If combined with higher economic growth, which can result from productivity gains through prioritization of capital spending, further fiscal buffers can be generated.

Figure 12: Palau Debt Service Requirements versus Fiscal Balance, Various Scenarios

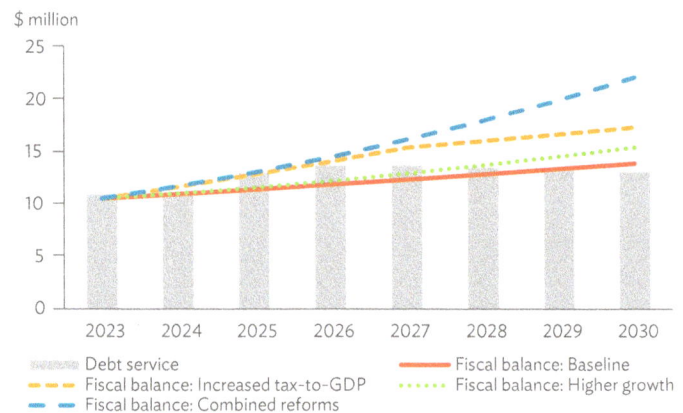

GDP = gross domestic product.
Source: Asian Development Bank estimates.

Palau's sound macro-fiscal policy framework, which helped achieve a rising tax-to-GDP ratio and a declining public wage bill prior to the severe exogenous shock brought on by COVID-19, can facilitate a quick return to fiscal surpluses upon economic recovery. However, further reforms will help generate additional fiscal space that, in turn, can support stronger recovery and more sustainable growth. Options include (i) tax reform that improves efficiency and equity of the tax system; (ii) reforming state-owned enterprises and social security funds to minimize the need for fiscal transfers; and (iii) prioritizing capital spending, both on timely infrastructure upgrades and regular maintenance of assets, to boost long-run productivity and growth, among others.

References

Graduate School USA. 2020. Assessing the impact of COVID-19 on the Palauan economy. *Economic Monitoring and Analysis Program (EconMAP) Technical Note*. https://pitiviti.org/news/downloads/EconFiscImpact_COVID-19_Mar2020_Web.pdf.

Graduate School USA. 2020. Where do we go from here? Updating the Economic Impact of COVID-19 and Strategies for Mitigation in the Republic of Palau. *Economic Monitoring and Analysis Program (EconMAP) Technical Note*. https://pitiviti.org/news/wp-content/uploads/downloads/2020/10/Palau_COVID_EconImpact_v2_Aug2020.pdf.

Papua New Guinea's expenditure strategy for recovery

Lead authors: Edward Faber and Magdelyn Kuari

The COVID-19 pandemic has heavily impacted the economy of Papua New Guinea (PNG), with GDP expected to contract by 2.9% in 2020. Lockdowns, restrictions imposed on international travel, and weaker international demand for PNG's exports have all impacted growth. Key sectors that are affected include construction, accommodation and food services, transport, and agriculture and forestry. In 2021, growth is seen to recover to 2.5%; however, growth will remain lackluster given the anticipated continuation of the pandemic and its impact on the international economy, including movement of people.

In 2020, the government has forecast revenues to fall by the equivalent of 2.9% of GDP compared with the 2019 outcome, and the fiscal deficit to widen to 8.2% of GDP. To support financing this wider deficit and maintain stimulus, bilateral and multilateral partners are assisting PNG, including ADB ($500 million), the International Monetary Fund ($363 million), and Australia ($100 million).

Ensuring quality of expenditure is fundamental for meaningful fiscal stimulus. Supporting capital projects, such as public infrastructure, through the capital budget provides much-needed economic stimulus, but there is a need to balance this with expenditure directed toward social support and service delivery. A supplementary budget in September 2020 focused on boosting capital expenditure, which increased to K6.3 billion compared with K5.9 billion under the original budget (Table 1). Although, operational expenditure was reduced from K12.7 billion to K11.6 billion, K1.2 billion was still allocated towards the country's response to COVID-19, including support for the health system; social programs; agricultural development and food security; micro, small, and medium-sized enterprises; and public infrastructure.

In the medium-term, the government has indicated that it will continue with its fiscal stimulus, increasing the overall share of capital expenditure. The 2021 budget projects a deficit of 7.6% of GDP in 2021, falling to 5.6% of GDP in 2022 and to 3.3% by 2023. In line with this, capital expenditure (Figure 13) remains on a growing path and is projected to reach 8.5% of GDP in 2021, compared with 7.9% of GDP under the 2020 supplementary budget, 7.2% in 2019, and 5.9% in 2018.

The Medium-Term Development Plan III 2018-2022 (MTDP III) outlines the government's plan for capital expenditure, with

Table 1: Papua New Guinea Expenditure Summary (K million)

Details	2020 Budget	2020 Supplementary Budget	2021 Budget
Total expenditure	18,726.5	17,989.3	19,607.8
Operating or recurrent budget	**12,746.0**	**11,599.8**	**12,136.7**
Compensation of employees	5,672.8	5,762.8	5,763.8
Debt service (interest payment and fees and charges)	2,156.9	2,064.4	2,270.8
Other operating (goods and services)	4,916.3	3772.6	4,102.1
Capital budget or Public Investment Program	**5,980.5**	**6,389.5**	**7,471.1**
Government of Papua New Guinea funded	3,683.4	4,092.4	4,824.4
Donor funded	932.1	932.1	1,008.3
Loan funded	1,365.0	1,365.0	1,638.4

Note: On 9 December 2020, the National Supreme Court ruled that the parliament meeting and its decisions on 17 November 2020 were unconstitutional, including the passing of the 2021 National Budget. The parliament will decide on re-tabling of the 2021 National Budget.

Source: Government of Papua New Guinea. 2020. 2021 National Budget. Port Moresby.

K27.2 billion planned for investment over 5 years, with large allocations to transport, utilities, economic sector investments, and to provinces. There are four broad components of capital expenditure: (i) the Public Investment Program (K1.7 billion in 2019); (ii) the Service Investment Program (K1.3 billion in 2019), which refers to funds allocated to provinces and districts; (iii) capital projects funded by grants received from development partners (K1.8 billion in 2019); and (iv) loans from development partners for capital projects (K1.3 billion in 2019). With a 2021 budget allocation of K7.5 billion for capital projects, this more than exceeds the MTDP III target of K5.8 billion for 2021, indicating the strong push for increased capital expenditure.

endorsed the expenditure rule in its staff-monitored program. Limiting the growth of personnel emoluments is central to achieving the overall downward path. In 2019, the government revived the Organizational, Staffing, and Personnel Emolument Audit Committee to examine the structure of payroll. In the 2020 national budget, the government announced several measures to try and contain growth in personnel emoluments, including (i) a plan to conduct an audit of the payroll by a third party; (ii) migrating all public servants onto a centralized government payroll system that incorporates the national identification registration; (iii) freezing further recruitment in nonessential areas; (iv) moving the payroll to operate within the government warranting system for central oversight; and (v) paying down the 4,000 individuals who remain on the government payroll, but have already reached retirement age. Although COVID-19 has affected the speed of implementation of these initiatives, progress is slowly advancing.

Figure 13: Papua New Guinea Trends in Capital and Operational Expenditure (2012–2021)

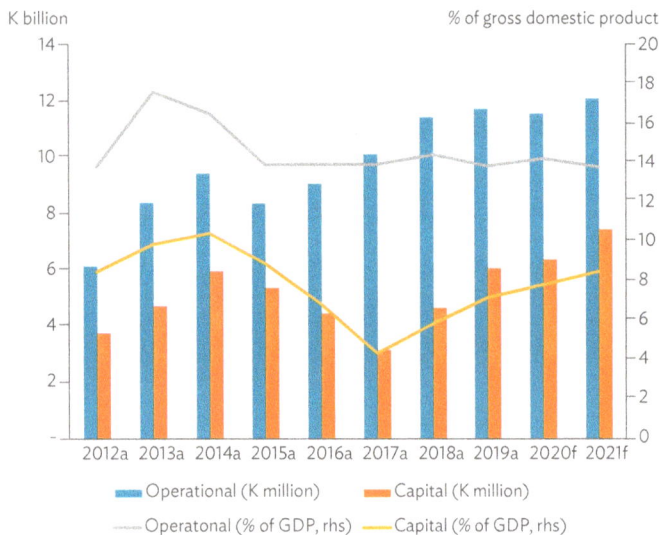

a= actual, f = forecast (Department of Treasury), GDP =gross domestic product, rhs = right-hand scale.
Source: Government of Papua New Guinea, Department of Treasury.

Figure 14: Papua New Guinea Trends in Operational Expenditure (2012-2021)

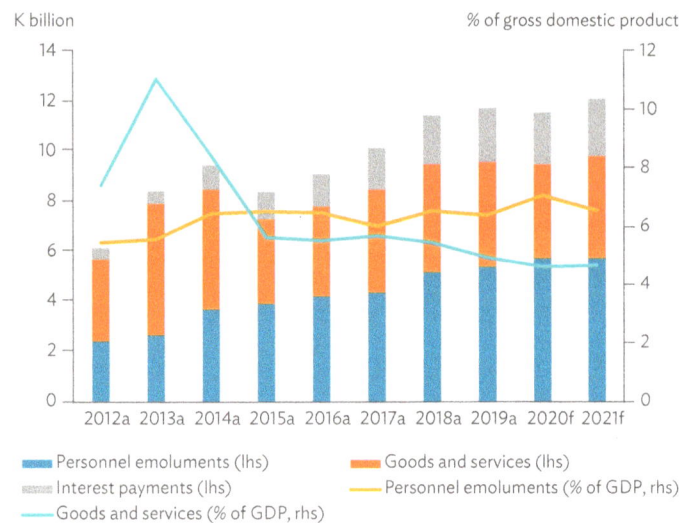

a= actual, f = forecast (Department of Treasury), GDP = gross domestic product, lhs = left-hand scale, rhs = right-hand scale.
Source: Government of Papua New Guinea, Department of Treasury.

Operational expenditure (Figure 13) has remained relatively stable at about 14% of GDP since 2015, notably falling from a peak of 17% in 2013 during a boom period. But personnel emoluments, which contributed 46% of total operational expenditure or 6.4% of GDP in 2019, have been growing as an overall share, expanding on average by 8% per year in real terms between 2012 and 2019. Consumption of goods and services, on the other hand, has fallen steadily from 54.0% of operational expenditure (equivalent to 7.4% of GDP) in 2012 to 35.6% of operational expenditure (5.0% of GDP) in 2019. Interest costs though have expanded, from 7.0% of total operational expenditure in 2012, to 18.3% in 2019, or from 1.0% of GDP in 2012 to 2.5% of GDP in 2020, as PNG's debt burden has increased.

The 2020 budget introduced an expenditure rule to reduce operational expenditure, excluding interest payments, from 18.7% of non-resource GDP in 2019 to 18.4% in 2021 and to 15.9% by 2024 (the 2021 budget modified these ratios only slightly, to 18.1% for 2021 and 15.7% for 2024). The International Monetary Fund

The overall expenditure strategy, with its focus on increasing capital expenditure and reining in operational expenditure, is sensible, though it will be important to ensure sufficient spending is maintained for social sectors, especially for the service delivery of health and education, which remain of central importance given the extra burdens imposed from the COVID-19 pandemic. The overall strategy of running a wider fiscal deficit is consistent with the approach taken by other economies to help stimulate growth and support recovery from COVID-19, but it will also contribute toward growing fiscal and debt sustainability challenges. To support a stronger and faster recovery, several other options can also be considered, including greater attention toward attracting foreign investment, working to advance large resource sector projects that are in the pipeline, and correcting the imbalance in foreign exchange with faster exchange rate depreciation.

Samoa and Tonga: opportunities in the storm?

Lead author: James Webb

To keep their populations safe from the COVID-19 pandemic, Samoa and Tonga have both maintained strict border controls. The high incidence of noncommunicable diseases within their populations and relatively weak local health systems make these countries particularly vulnerable to the health impacts of the pandemic, and closing the borders undoubtedly saved lives that would have been lost if there had been uncontrolled community transmission. However, COVID-19 presents a different type of crisis, with the impacts becoming more severe the longer the borders remain closed. Labor opportunities beyond the border may present a short term opportunity to provide relief to worker and household incomes, and potentially reduce the pressure on government fiscal positions.

A DIFFERENT TYPE OF CRISIS TO PUSH TOURISM TO THE BRINK

Like most countries in the Pacific, the closure of international borders has protected Samoa and Tonga from the health impacts of the pandemic, but has also eliminated international tourism as a pillar of the economy. Prior to the pandemic, tourism receipts had grown from 17.3% of GDP in Samoa in fiscal year 2012 (FY2012, ended 30 June) to 23.1% by FY2019. Tourism receipts in Tonga stayed relatively flat over the same period, reaching 9.7% by FY2019 (also ended 30 June) (Figure 15). Direct tourism employment supports around one-third of all jobs in Samoa and contributes to the income of one-third of all households in Tonga, suggesting that the decline of the industry threatens to reverse development gains.[1] In the case of Tonga, a recent business survey by the Tonga Chamber of Commerce and Industry indicates that over 60% of firms have reduced the number of staff and/or workers' hours in response to the economic downturn, suggesting that the impacts of the border closures have well and truly begun to impact on the labor market.

Samoa and Tonga are frequently exposed to natural hazards and their associated impact on local livelihoods. In the case of tropical cyclones, strength (e.g., wind speed) is often the key determinant of damages to the community and the tourism industry, with prevention and reconstruction efforts typically increasing overall economic activities. However, COVID-19 and the control measures used to ensure community safety present a dramatically different profile to a relatively short-lived natural hazard. The daily impact of the border closures are well understood, but the duration of the crisis has become the key determinant of the severity of the economic downturn, as businesses are required to draw down on equity (or accumulate debt) to meet fixed costs—even those who have temporarily ceased operations. During the measles crisis in Samoa, partial mitigation measures (such as allowing entry only to those who had been vaccinated for measles) limited the depth of the economic crisis by keeping borders open, and a mass vaccination campaign effectively limited the duration of the impact by immunizing the local population. With no vaccine in hand, both Samoan and Tongan authorities rightly recognized the vulnerability of their populations. A similar strategy to measles is clearly not viable for addressing COVID-19 risks, at least until an effective vaccine is widely available.

It was assumed in the *Asian Development Outlook 2020 Update* that travel to Samoa and Tonga would recommence after July 2021. However, with no discussions underway with either Australia or New Zealand for a partial reopening, it is difficult to see how Samoa and Tonga will reopen borders in the immediate future. This leaves the tourism industry in a difficult position to plan for an eventual recovery. In Samoa, the extended slowdown in tourism from the combined measles and COVID-19 crises will mean that tourism operators may be without international patrons for almost two full years, while in Tonga, 18 months of no tourists and damage from tropical cyclone Harold could push many operators to close down. Few companies could continue without revenue for such a prolonged period or (in the case of Tonga) put aside enough capital to repair and reinvest in their properties without sacrificing their operating balances. In such an environment, the resulting degradation of both physical capital and private sector balance sheets may persist well beyond the end of any shutdown period.

The previous investments of local superannuation funds will buffer some of the key tourism properties from closing their doors permanently in order to protect against capital losses to the respective funds. But smaller operators will not benefit from private equity injections while the global tourism industry is facing an unprecedented and simultaneous downturn. It is also unclear that the local industries in either country will be open in time to make use of a "post-lockdown" surge in expected South Pacific tourism if these countries are among the slower of the subregional destinations to reopen. International competition in tourism markets may be fierce once a vaccine is widely available, and there could be significant first-mover advantages within the Pacific to those with established, safe, and contained travel arrangements.

Figure 15: Samoa and Tonga Tourism Receipts

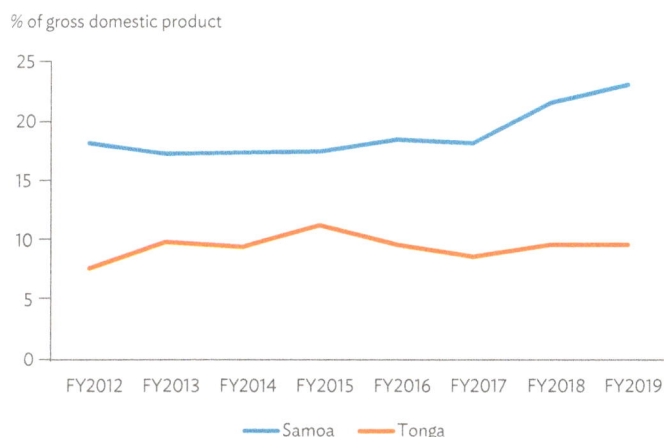

% of gross domestic product

FY = fiscal year.
Source: International Monetary Fund Article IV Staff Report, various years.

GOVERNMENTS STEP IN

Given the importance of preserving the ability to recover quickly post-COVID-19, both governments have responded with stimulus packages to support the local economy. In Tonga, the government approved a $26.1 million COVID-19 economic and social stimulus package (equivalent to 5.2% of GDP) to mitigate the economic and social damage, and Samoa approved $55.9 million (equivalent to 6.9% of GDP).

In addition to other direct transfers to vulnerable groups and allowing partial withdrawals from superannuation, both packages funded a wage subsidy to support firms in retaining employees by temporarily lowering the cost of wages or a form of unemployment payment for those who lose their jobs. In supporting the continuation of the employer-employee relationship, the wage subsidy can help to mitigate the ongoing effects associated with unemployment, while complementing policies directed at helping firms manage a period of inactivity or significant disruptions to production. Both countries made their respective programs available to anyone who lost employment or had reduced hours of work because of the crises, with both formal and informal sector workers eligible. In Tonga for example, wage subsidies have been provided to 5,326 affected workers across 673 businesses—representing over 13% of the total labor force. The corresponding target range in Samoa was between 3,000 and 6,500 workers.

There has also been a series of grants credit programs to support business cash positions and continuity. The Government of Tonga provided financial assistance to over 2,100 formal and informal businesses to support business continuity at a cost of around $7.1 million, with payments depending on the annual turnover of the firm. Around 20% of the funds were allocated to firms in each of the primary and manufacturing sectors, and 60% for firms in the services sector, including tourism. Likewise, Samoa reduced electricity charges for the tourism sector, and provided reduced rents to businesses located on government properties.

The financial systems of both countries were relatively stable prior to the crisis, with adequate liquidity and nonperforming loans within acceptable limits (for example, nonperforming loans were only 3.9% of total loans in Samoa prior to the crisis). However, the governments have recognized the possible strain that short term liquidity constraints may place on the local banking system, especially to those institutions exposed to tourism sector lending. The COVID-19-related shock to the real economy could be compounded by a simultaneous financial sector shock as banks seek to shore up their balance sheets. Small and medium-sized enterprises in the tourism sector would be most vulnerable to this de-risking, and this could further constrain companies' ability to expand their operations when demand returns. In response, public banking institutions have also been called on to provide additional assistance, in addition to encouraging local commercial banks to allow for interest-only payment periods and repayment holidays.

In Tonga, the successful Government Development Loan (GDL) revolving fund, administered by the Tonga Development Bank,

has been extended for another 5 years.[2] The government has also provided an additional $2.2 million under the GDL facility to deliver concessional credit targeted predominantly to the tourism sector. The additional financing will be provided via loans of up to $220,000 at 3% interest for a maturity of up to 5 years, enabling a significant pool of short-term liquidity for affected businesses.

In Samoa, the government has covered 2 percentage points of all business interest costs at commercial banks over a 3-month period, 3 months of loan repayments for all small businesses under the Government Guarantee Schemes (administered by the Samoa Business Hub), and 2 months of interest payments for all loans with the Development Bank of Samoa (DBS). A potential risk to the government is the guarantee provided to the DBS for the credit line facility put in place in the aftermath of cyclone Evan. The existing portfolio is already highly exposed to the tourism sector: of the 19% nonperforming debt in the total portfolio, tourism-centered loans account for nearly half (International Monetary Fund 2020). With its balance sheet already under pressure, it is unclear how much additional support DBS can provide without additional equity or cash injections from the government.

Together, the government packages have undoubtedly provided a partial buffer against the significant fall in household incomes and business continuity, but have put severe strain on fiscal resources. With the borders unlikely to reopen until well into 2021, domestic economic conditions will continue to deteriorate. It is clear that subsequent rounds of government stimulus will be needed to support household incomes and business continuity, which will put fiscal resources under further strain.

OPPORTUNITIES BEYOND BORDERS

Although the tourism sector will remain sluggish until a vaccine is widely distributed, remittances may provide an opportunity to alleviate domestic economic pressures.

Among Pacific countries, Samoa and Tonga are notable for their large remittances flows relative to the size of their economies. In Tonga, remittances were an estimated 29.4% of GDP (FY2018), and an estimated 23.4% of GDP (FY2019) in Samoa (Figure 16). Any reduction in remittances stemming from travel restrictions or recessions in source markets could unwind recent development gains and deepen the poverty gap (ADB 2020a and 2020b). In Tonga, around 20% of average household income are directly tied to remittances and four out of five houses receive remitted income.

In the aftermath of crisis such as cyclones, Samoan and Tongan remittances are generally robust, with families often sending more money home to help rebuild or cover for lost incomes and crops. COVID-19 was expected to be similar in the short term, but the labor markets of remitting countries were viewed as the key risks as the crisis continues and labor outcomes potentially deteriorate. This was particularly true given that the diaspora in Australia and New Zealand is around 6 times larger than the seasonal worker contingent for Tonga, and around 24 times larger for Samoa, and that diaspora are more likely to be highly exposed to general economic conditions in foreign labor markets.[3] However, remittances in both Tonga and Samoa have held up more than expected, with remittances in Samoa increasing 6.2% in the 12 months to September, and remittances in Tonga being largely unchanged in FY2020 compared with FY2019.

Figure 16: Samoa and Tonga Overseas Remittances

$ million

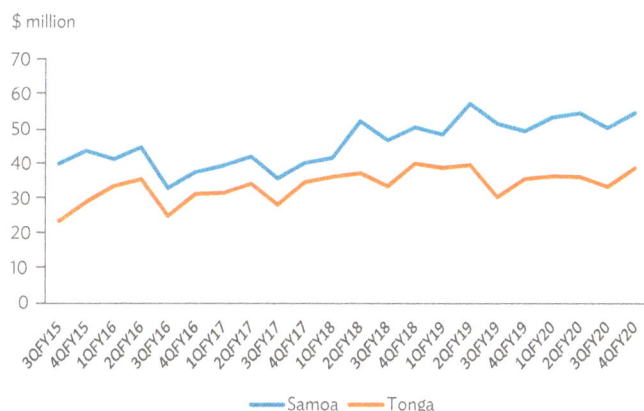

FY = fiscal year, Q = quarter.
Sources: Central Bank of Samoa and National Reserve Bank of Tonga.

Continued remittance income has supported local income and consumption, alleviating pressure from government stimulus, and supporting revenue from consumption taxation. However, the risks remain elevated, especially given the complications of mobilizing new cohorts for the upcoming summer harvests. For example, between March and October, no Tongan workers entered or left Australia because of complete closure of the borders. As at the end of October, 285 new workers have arrived from Tonga under the Seasonal Workers Program, but 81 workers had returned (including 1 from the Pacific Labour Scheme) and a further 200 workers are estimated to be on waiting lists to also return home. In New Zealand at the start of October, there were about 1,259 Samoans under the Recognised Seasonal Employment (RSE) scheme ahead of the summer picking season (down from 2,234 at the end of the season in May 2020), while 487 Tongan RSE workers are due to return home from the 1,634 currently abroad (as compared to a total of 1,607 in May 2020) (Summerfruit New Zealand 2020).

As of November, an estimated 6,500 RSE workers will still be in New Zealand, about 1,000 more RSE workers than in November 2019 (5,675). But by March 2021, there would normally be at least another 5,500 RSE workers in New Zealand for the peak apple harvest (Bedford 2020). With the border only partially open, it is unclear if this figure will be reached. In addition to potentially fewer seasonal workers, 70,000 backpackers would typically be in New Zealand over the summer months that could be drawn on for orchard and vineyard work. That number is down to approximately 11,000 currently, with no new backpackers likely to feature in the South Pacific for at least another year. Similarly, Australia's fruit and vegetable farmers may need an extra 26,000 workers to harvest their crops this summer.[4] Such large shortages in critical labor could result in domestic food price volatility, or declines in export

income, at a time when New Zealand and Australian households and governments are particularly exposed. New Zealand has already opened an RSE intake of an additional 2,000 placements to meet the anticipated labor shortfall, requiring employers to pay for the quarantine period, but there will be significant demand for further seasonal workers.[5]

While any move to safely reopen *inbound* travel to Samoa and Tonga should be pursued when the countries are ready and willing, an interim step of smoothing barriers for *outbound* seasonal labor schemes may present an unlikely opportunity to capitalize on acute labor shortages in Australia and New Zealand in markets where Samoan and Tongan labor have a demonstrated track record. The COVID-19-contained status of both Samoa and Tonga should facilitate relatively smooth border processing, and the delay on returning cohorts should give authorities enough time to plan for possible quarantine or self-isolation on their return— something which may not even be necessary if Australia and New Zealand maintain their record on managing the pandemic. Such arrangements would reduce the pressure on the island governments to support household incomes in the absence of tourism demand, while also allowing them space to meet the possible thresholds for contained travel arrangements—if and when they feel they are prepared to take that risk.

Ultimately, pushing hard to expand the seasonal worker schemes for the upcoming season would substantially alleviate the economic and fiscal pressures facing Samoa and Tonga, without exposing domestic populations and health systems to the threat of COVID-19 from inbound tourism. For Australia and New Zealand, it would also meet a substantial labor shortage in key agricultural industries, avoiding possible food price inflation or a fall in exports—although the window for action is closing quickly. Therefore, it is in everyone's interest to take the first steps to resume more regular travel in the subregion as soon as possible.

Endnotes

[1] Estimates provided by ADB.

[2] An independent review of the GDL Scheme highlighted the critical role the program has played in extending access to credit to micro, small, and medium-sized enterprises that would otherwise be underserved by the domestic banking sector. The report notes the relatively low level of nonperforming loans under the GDL (5.0% in FY2019, although it increased to 8.0% in FY2020 because of the impacts of the dual shocks on firms' liquidity), demonstrating the effectiveness of the Tonga Development Bank screening, selection, and monitoring protocols.

[3] Temporary worker figures taken from FY2019 estimates of participants in the Recognised Seasonal Employment Program (New Zealand), Seasonal Worker Program (Australia), and Pacific Labour Scheme (Australia) (Tonga: 5,838; Samoa: 3,162) as compared with 2013 estimates of diaspora in both Australia and New Zealand (Tonga: 33,667; Samoa: 75,540).

4   Report by Ernst & Young, as cited by K. Sullivan. 2020. *Coronavirus restrictions could lead to 26,000-person shortfall for coming harvests, report says*. ABC News, 30 September 2020; https://www.abc.net.au/news/2020-09-30/coronavirus-farm-worker-shortage-coming-harvests/12714694.

5   PACNEWS. 2020. *NZ Govt to allow 2000 horticulture workers in from Pacific under strict conditions*. 27 November 2020. http://www.pina.com.fj/index.php?p=pacnews&m=read&o=14781742615fc08350ac0b4afa1657.

References

ADB. 2020a. *Proposed Countercyclical Support Facility Grant to the Independent State of Samoa: Health Expenditure and Livelihoods Support Program*. Manila.

ADB. 2020b. *Report and Recommendation of the President: Proposed Policy-Based Grant to the Kingdom of Tonga: Strengthening Macroeconomic Resilience Program*. Manila.

Bedford, C. 2020. *New Zealand's seasonal labour shortage: why local workers aren't enough*. https://devpolicy.org/new-zealands-seasonal-labour-shortage-why-local-workers-arent-enough-20201124/ (accessed 26 November 2020).

International Monetary Fund. 2020. *Samoa: Staff Concluding Statement of the 2020 Article IV Mission* https://www.imf.org/en/News/Articles/2020/03/02/mcs030220-samoa-staff-concluding-statement-of-the-2020-article-iv-mission (accessed 26 November 2020).

Summerfruit New Zealand. 2020. *Pacific Repatriations–Country Overview*. https://www.summerfruitnz.co.nz/assets/News/Pacific-Repatriations-8-Oct.pdf (accessed 26 November 2020).

Supporting a sustainable recovery in Solomon Islands

Lead authors: Jacqueline Connell and Prince Cruz

Solomon Islands reported its first case of COVID-19 in October. By 24 November, cases had grown to 17, mostly among repatriated students and athletes in quarantine. Fortunately, no community transmission was reported, indicating the critical role that testing and quarantine have played in containing the virus.

The government implemented containment and health preparedness measures following the Cabinet's declaration of the State of Public Emergency along with the approval of the COVID-19 Preparedness and Response Plan (with funding equivalent to 1.1% of GDP) in March. The State of Public Emergency has been extended further to March 2021.

To help protect jobs and reduce the economic impact of COVID-19, the government announced an Economic Stimulus Package (ESP) in May worth SI$309 million, equivalent to 2.5% of GDP (Government of Solomon Islands 2020) (Figure 17). The ESP has five main components:

- **Economic continuity measures (SI$25 million).** These measures include electricity tariff subsidies to households and businesses, domestic port charges waiver, tax relief, bank loan and interest repayment relief, small and medium-sized enterprises (SMEs) rental relief, grants to provincial health authorities, and withdrawal allowances to National Provident Fund members.
- **Crop production support (SI$70 million).** The support includes price and freight subsidies for copra and cocoa. Farmers producing other crops, including noni, kava, cassava, and taro, are also given cash grants and equipment support.
- **Forestry, fisheries, and tourism sector support (SI$ 44 million) and loans to SMEs (SI$10 million).** Fisheries and timber producers are provided cash grants and equipment to increase production and sales. Cash grants are also extended to tourism marketing agencies. Concessional loans are extended by the Development Bank of Solomon Islands to rural SMEs, focusing on crop production, fisheries, and tourism to boost employment and exports.
- **Support to state-owned enterprises (SOEs) and large employers (SI$70 million).** Equity injections to SOEs to ensure their operations continue despite the impacts of the pandemic. The main beneficiaries are Solomon Airlines, Development Bank of Solomon Islands, Solomon Water, and SolTuna. Large private companies that are major employers are assisted through export credit, or liquidity support through the banking system.
- **Infrastructure investment (SI$90 million).** These projects include roads and wharves (SI$39 million), bridges (SI$30 million), and airports (SI$21 million).

Figure 17: Solomon Islands Economic Stimulus Package

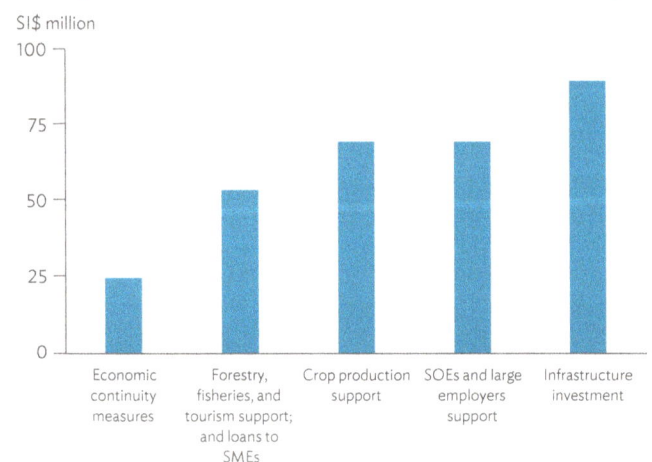

SMEs = small and medium-sized enterprises, SOE = state-owned enterprise.
Source: Government of Solomon Islands. 2020. *Economic Stimulus Package to Address the Impacts of the COVID-19 Pandemic*. Honiara.

About 40% of the ESP is targeted to farmers, forestry, fisheries, and tourism. Much of this spending will support rural households, whose average income was less than half that of urban households before COVID-19, based on the 2012/2013 Household Income and Expenditure Survey (Government of Solomon Islands 2015).

Another vulnerable group is formal sector workers who tend to face higher costs of living in urban areas and whose jobs may be affected by COVID-19. This includes workers in the capital, Honiara, where most wards had poverty rates above the national average before COVID-19 (Government of Solomon Islands 2017). The government's support to SOEs and large employers, as well as electricity tariff subsidies, and rental and loan repayment relief, will help these urban households.

Even with this support, the government's ability to directly target the poorest and most vulnerable has been constrained by its limited social protection system. The widely scattered population also creates challenges for delivering government support and services.

Solomon Island's economic stimulus package is smaller as a share of GDP and per capita expenditure when compared with COVID-19 spending announced by other Pacific countries (Figure 18). Several countries have announced additional COVID-19 spending in their 2021 budgets. However, the Government of Solomon Islands' budget will be considered by Parliament in the first quarter of 2021.

Figure 18: COVID-19 Spending Package, as of November 2020

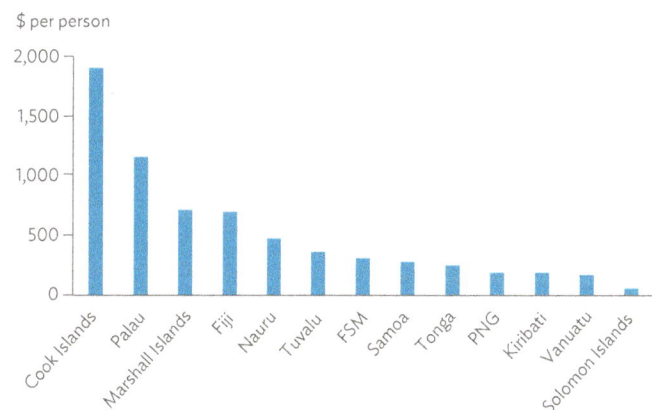

COVID-19 = coronavirus disease, FSM = Federated States of Micronesia, PNG = Papua New Guinea.
Note: As stated in the background paper, "The policy database might not fully reflect all the measures implemented by the economies considered. The policy database includes publicly available information and its intent is solely to inform the public, and it does not make any judgment."
Source: Asian Development Bank COVID-19 Policy Database. https://covid19policy.adb.org/ (accessed 18 November 2020).

The government is financing the ESP through the issuance of COVID-19 domestic bonds, support from development partners, and budget reallocations. The government did not have significant savings from previous fiscal surpluses that it could draw on to finance the ESP. Fiscal deficits were recorded in 3 of the last 4 years and government's cash on hand was equivalent to 0.8 months of recurrent spending in 2019 (International Monetary Fund 2020).

The government estimated that total financing secured for the COVID-19 response was equivalent to 5.0% of GDP. While above the value of the ESP, this financing will help offset the expected fall in revenue, especially from taxes and export duties because of COVID-19.

With Solomon Islands having the second highest ratio of merchandise exports to GDP in any Pacific developing member country, the economy has been vulnerable to disruption in exports markets. The 25.9% fall in logging output during the second quarter of the year was accompanied by a 22.6% fall in the value of logging exports, which are mostly to the People's Republic of China (Figure 19). This will have reduced government revenue from export duties, which supplied almost a fifth of the domestic revenue over the last 5 years. Further ahead, a potential uptick in exports, supported by a nascent recovery in the People's Republic of China, could help ease fiscal and economic pressures.

Figure 19: Solomon Islands Log Output and Exports

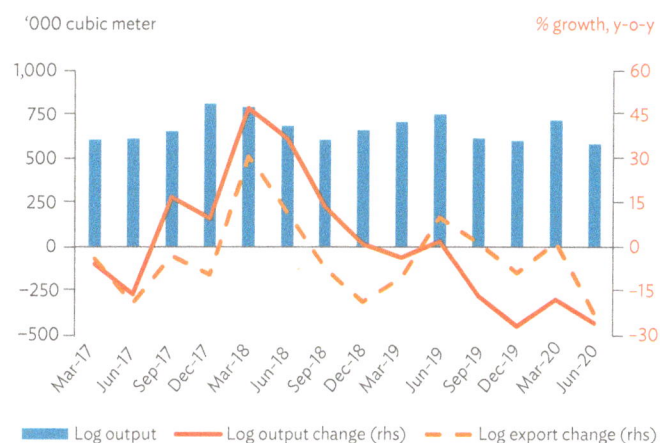

rhs = right-hand scale, y-o-y = year-on-year.
Note: Log exports based on value in local currency.
Source: Asian Development Bank estimates using data from the Central Bank of Solomon Islands.

Despite the increase in government borrowing in the second and third quarters of 2020, public debt remained relatively low, equivalent to 11.6% of GDP in September 2020 (Figure 20). While this provides some space to absorb the external shock of COVID-19, public debt is expected to rise to finance expansionary fiscal policy and infrastructure investments over the medium term. The IMF (2020) projects that the ratio of public debt to GDP will rise to 29.0% in 2025, from 8.4% in 2019, although the risk of debt distress remains moderate.

Beyond the immediate fiscal response to the pandemic, targeted efforts will be needed to improve fiscal buffers, and ensure that revenue mobilization is efficient.

Figure 20: Solomon Islands National Government Debt

% of gross domestic product

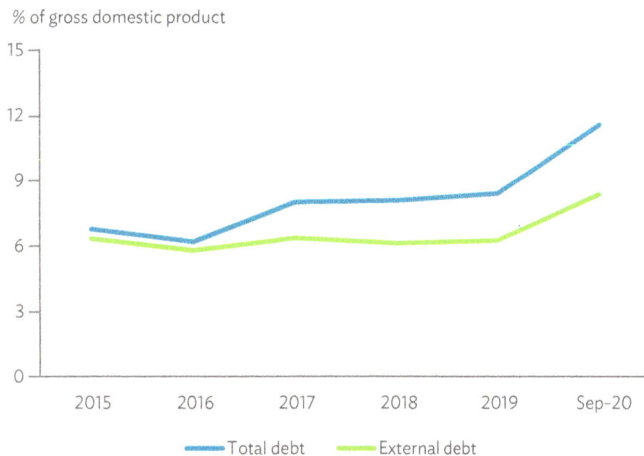

Source: Asian Development Bank estimates using data from Solomon Islands Debt Report, Ministry of Finance and Treasury, various years.

The current tax system of Solomon Islands is complex, expensive to administer, includes distortionary exemptions, and relies on high rates applied to a narrow base, which discourages compliance. Getting the tax system right is important as the government seeks higher levels of productive investment to support job creation and sustainable growth.

Prior to COVID-19, the government embarked on a tax review to deliver a fair, simple, and broad-based tax system. There are plans to introduce a value-added tax to replace various goods taxes, sales tax, stamp duties, and customs duties that currently have multiple rates of tax, and different rules and procedures. Building consensus and capacity for reform will be critical alongside strengthening revenue administration to support the economic recovery ahead.

References

Government of Solomon Islands. 2015. *Solomon Islands 2012/13 Household Income and Expenditure Survey (HIES) National Analytical Report (Volume 1)*. Honiara.

Government of Solomon Islands. 2017. *Solomon Islands Poverty Maps Based on the 2012/13 Household Income and Expenditure Survey and the 2009 Population and Housing Census*. Honiara.

Government of Solomon Islands. 2020. *Economic Stimulus Package to Address the Impacts of the COVID-19 Pandemic*. Honiara.

International Monetary Fund. 2020. Solomon Islands: Requests for Purchase Under the Rapid Financing Instrument and Disbursement Under the Rapid Credit Facility. *IMF Country Report* No. 20/190. Washington, DC.

Vanuatu: Responding to immediate and midterm recovery needs

Lead authors: Jacqueline Connell and Prince Cruz

The Government of Vanuatu entered 2020 in a strong fiscal position and has responded to COVID-19 and Tropical Cyclone (TC) Harold with health and economic stimulus measures. But, with the cost of recovery estimated larger still, and travel restrictions continuing to halt tourism, fiscal pressures could mount in 2021.

Vanuatu reported its first COVID-19 case in early November after one of the more than 2,250 people repatriated tested positive while in quarantine. Containment measures, enacted under the declaration of a state of emergency, were intensified. All travel from the island of Efate, location of the capital Port Vila, was temporarily restricted on top of the international travel restrictions that were in place since March 2020. The quarantine period for repatriated individuals was temporarily extended from 14 days to 28 days.

The economy is projected to contract in 2020 because of the combined impacts of COVID-19 and TC Harold that hit the country in April. The Government of Vanuatu estimated in their October Post-Disaster Needs Assessment that the combined losses of TC Harold and COVID-19 would be equivalent to 68.7% of GDP. Most of this impact is because of TC Harold losses, including infrastructure damage, while 18% is because of economic losses from COVID-19 for the period March–June (Table 2). Yet, economic losses from COVID-19 will likely reach well beyond this, given that border closures continue to restrict international tourism.

The government has launched the Vanuatu Recover Strategy 2020–2023, *Yumi Evriwan Tugeta*, to coordinate a medium term response. The strategy is aimed at restoring and strengthening essential public services, supporting livelihoods and economic recovery, and repairing public and private infrastructure. It estimates the cost of recovery and restoration from TC Harold and COVID-19 at Vt36.4 billion, the equivalent of 36.8% of Vanuatu's 2020 GDP (Figure 21). The strategy indicates this financing could come from the government, the private sector, and development partners.

The government's immediate fiscal response to COVID-19 has comprised two key components totaling 5.2% of GDP (Vt5.1 billion). These are the:

- **Health Preparedness and Response Plan (0.8% of GDP).** Approved in January, the Health Preparedness and Response Plan was designed to prevent COVID-19 from reaching Vanuatu and prevent local transmission if it did.
- **Economic Stimulus Program (4.4% of GDP).** Approved in April, the economic stimulus program aims to alleviate the social and economic impacts of COVID-19. Key components include:
  - » **Employment stabilization payments.** The government reimbursed businesses affected by COVID-19 up to Vt30,000 per employee each month for up to 4 months.

As a further incentive to retain workers, employers received 12% of the amount they were reimbursed for wages under this payment to cover both employer and employee contributions to the Vanuatu National Provident Fund (VNPF) and administrative costs. The program closed in September.

» **Small and medium-sized enterprises grants.** The government provides a cash grant of Vt60,000 to businesses with an annual turnover of Vt200 million or less.
» **Tuition fee grants.** The government provides grants to schools to exempt households from paying tuition fees for early childhood care, and primary and secondary education.
» **Tax and fee exemptions.** The government provides exemptions for (i) residence and work permit fees to encourage nonresidents to remain in Vanuatu, (ii) road tax to support businesses and individuals, (iii) rental tax to support property owners, and (iv) business license fees in 2020.
» **Agriculture support.** The government provides price subsidies and transportation assistance from farms to urban centers to support farmers. It will also support the production and marketing of copra, kava, and other crops.

Figure 21: Government of Vanuatu Estimates of Tropical Cyclone Harold and COVID-19 Impact and Recovery Spending

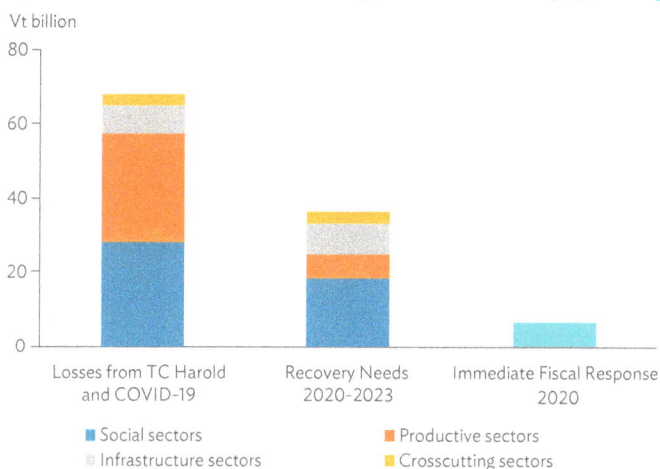

COVID-19 = coronavirus disease, TC = tropical cyclone.
Sources: Government of Vanuatu. 2020. *Post-Disaster Needs Assessment TC Harold & COVID-19. Volume A and B.* Port Vila; Government of Vanuatu. 2020. *Yumi Evriwan Tugeta: Vanuatu Recovery Strategy 2020-2023.* Port Vila; and Department of Finance and Treasury budget documents.

Further, the government authorized hardship loans from the VNPF to members. Between March and May, when the facility was stopped, about 20,000 loans were made. The loans comprised an interest-free withdrawal from a member's account for 6 months of up to Vt100,000. After 6 months, the member can either pay the plan with interest or permanently withdraw the funds with a penalty.

Vanuatu achieved fiscal surpluses in the 2 years prior to 2020, enabling it to a build a fiscal cash buffer against shocks. Even so, the continued contraction in tourism, combined with lower demand because of containment, will reduce tax revenue while the stimulus program increases expenditure. The resulting fiscal deficit in 2020 is expected to be financed through domestic resources and development partner assistance.

Further ahead, additional stimulus will be required if the pandemic continues and Vanuatu will face increasing fiscal pressure. Although recovery measures are ongoing, two of the stimulus measures designed to support formal sector workers have closed: the Employment Stabilization Program and the VNPF withdrawal facility. The government may face increased pressure to support affected businesses and households if travel restrictions continue to prevent tourism through 2021.

There are risks also to the sustainability of the Honorary Citizenship Program as a source of revenue. Revenues from the Honorary Citizenship Program increased by 32.5% year-on-year in the first 6 months of 2020 to supply 43.4% of government revenue. A possible reduction in foreign demand or accessibility for the Honorary Citizenship Program, in combination with subdued tax revenues, would increase fiscal pressures in 2021.

External borrowing is constrained by the government's Debt Management Strategy (2019–2022), which targets nominal external debt to be below 40% of GDP and public debt below 60% of GDP. External debt approached this ceiling in 2019 despite strong debt repayment, including early repayment of some loans (Figure 22). If the economy contracts significantly because of the combined impact of TC Harold and COVID-19, external debts would need to be retired, possibly financed by domestic debt, to keep the ratio of debt to GDP within the ceiling.

Figure 22: Vanuatu Government Debt

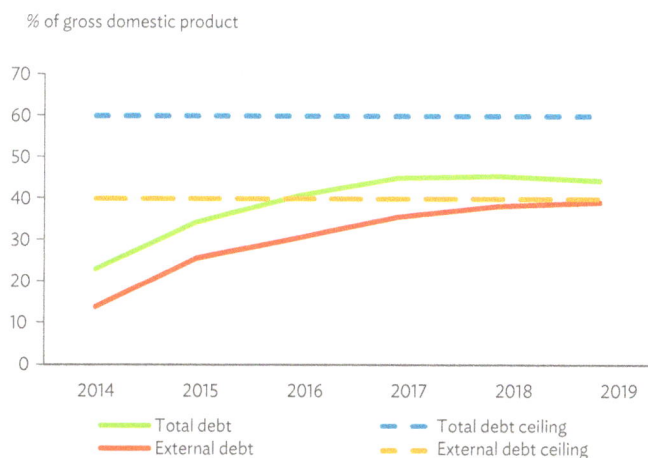

Source: Asian Development Bank estimates using data from the Reserve Bank of Vanuatu.

Table 2: Government of Vanuatu Estimated Impacts of Tropical Cyclone Harold and COVID-19, and Recovery Needs

	Estimated Effects of TC Harold and COVID-19 (Vt million)				Recovery Needs 2020–2023 (Vt million)		
	Damage	COVID-19 Losses	TC Harold Losses	Total Effects	Short Term	Medium Term	Total
Social Sectors	**18,839**	**3,790**	**5,405**	**28,035**	**5,409**	**12,920**	**18,328**
Housing	10,001	-	342	10,343	1,766	909	2,675
Health and nutrition	1,870	73	256	2,199	3,024	8,759	11,783
Education	6,259	824	29	7,112	-	2,934	2,934
Culture	436	-	-	436	347	160	507
Justice and community service	274	2,893	4,778	7,945	272	157	429
Productive Sectors	**2,844**	**7,845**	**18,707**	**29,396**	**3,517**	**3,098**	**6,615**
Food security and agriculture	1,158	266	18,131	19,555	2,952	2,158	5,110
Businesses and tourism	1,686	7,579	576	9,841	565	940	1,505
Infrastructure Sectors	**5,972**	**383**	**1,242**	**7,597**	**4,564**	**3,643**	**8,206**
Public buildings	396	3	10	409	458	23	481
Transport	2,827	316	81	3,224	1,038	2,497	3,536
Water, sanitation, and hygiene	1,984	29	319	2,333	1,534	309	1,843
Energy	168	-	10	178	10	800	810
Telecommunications	597	35	821	1,454	1,523	13	1,536
Crosscutting sectors	**32**	**10**	**2,978**	**3,021**	**947**	**2,331**	**3,278**
Disaster risk management	32	10	2,978	3,021	-	1,000	1,000
Environment	-	-	-	-	947	1,330	2,277
Total	**27,688**	**12,028**	**28,332**	**68,048**	**14,436**	**21,991**	**36,428**

- = no value, COVID-19 = coronavirus disease, TC = tropical cyclone.
Notes: Economic losses for COVID-19 are estimated for the period March–June 2020. Total figures on damage and losses do not include the disaster effects on the environment sector. The gender and social inclusion sector did not present a monetary assessment of disaster effects.
Sources: Government of Vanuatu. 2020. *Post-Disaster Needs Assessment TC Harold & COVID-19. Volume A and B.* Port Vila; *Yumi Evriwan Tugeta:* Vanuatu Recovery Strategy 2020–2023; and Department of Finance and Treasury budget documents.

Toward a gender-inclusive response to the COVID-19 crisis: insights from the latest census in the Federated States of Micronesia

The economy of the Federated States of Micronesia (FSM) is estimated to have contracted by 5.4% in fiscal year (FY) 2020 (ended 30 September) and projected to decline by a further 1.8% in FY2021, mainly because of the effects of COVID-19. As the country charts its path to recovery, findings from the most recent census, the 2016 Integrated Agriculture Census (2016 IAC), provide a baseline to consider what the gender-differentiated impacts of COVID-19 may be and an insight into gender-responsive recovery in the short and medium terms.

The population is shrinking, with women and young families leaving

Total population reported in the 2016 IAC was 87,357, 15.5% lower than the reported 103,382 in the 2014 Household Income and Expenditure Survey (Figure 1). The FSM's peak population was reported in the 2000 census with 107,008, which declined by 3.9% to 102,839 in 2010.[1]

Figure 1: Federated States of Micronesia Population, by Gender

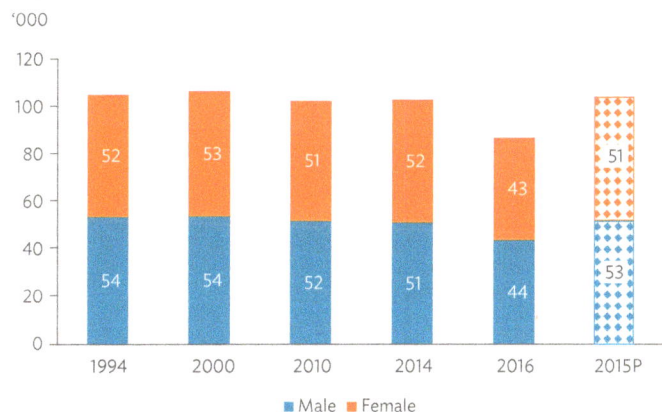

p = projection from FSM Statistics.
Sources: FSM Statistics Integrated Agriculture Census 2016 and 2010 Census of Population and Housing.

The decline in the population from 2000 to 2010 was attributed to economic stagnation experienced in that decade, which gave people a strong incentive to migrate to the United States mainland, Hawaii, Guam, and the Commonwealth of the Northern Mariana Islands.[2] A survey of FSM migrants in the United States show that there are more women migrants from the FSM than men (53:47).

The main reasons for migrating were employment, family reasons, and education (IOM 2016). Economic contraction induced by COVID-19 may lead to further decline in the population in the medium term and may have implications for development of a skilled, diverse, and inclusive workforce.

When broken down by age group, the biggest declines in population were seen among children (age below 15) and young adults (15–29 years old) (Figure 2). The combined population aged below 30 fell by 17.8% from 2014 to 2016, whereas the population of older adults (30-59 years old) fell by only 13.2%. The share of children fell to 32% of the total population in 2016, down from 46% in 1989 and 40% in 2000. This implies that young workers and families are migrating at a faster rate compared with other age groups, likely in search of economic and academic opportunities (IOM 2016).

Figure 2: Federated States of Micronesia Population, by Age Group

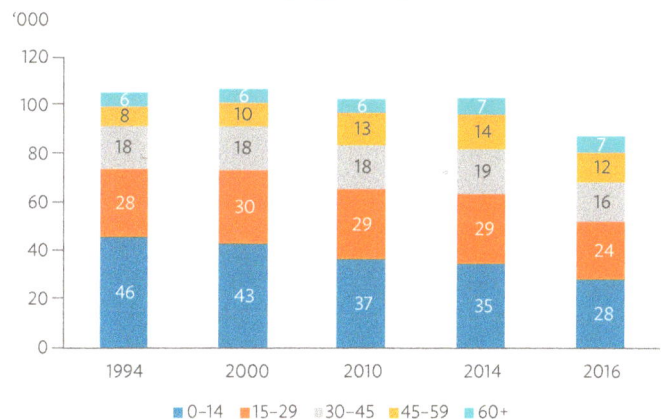

Sources: FSM Statistics Integrated Agriculture Census 2016 and 2010 Census of Population and Housing.

All four states reported population declines, with Chuuk's, the most populous state, falling by almost 20% from 48,654 in 2010 to 39,350 in 2016 (Figure 3). The population of Pohnpei, location of the capital Palikir, fell by 14% (from 36,196 to 31,159); that of Kosrae by 12% and the population of Yap declined by only 3%. Chuuk's share of the national population continued its decline, accounting for only 45% in 2016 (down from 51% in 1980). Pohnpei's share, on the other hand, continued to rise to 36% in 2016 from 30% in 1980. The shares of Yap (12%) and Kosrae (7%) remained relatively stable from 1980.

Figure 3: Federated States of Micronesia Population, by State

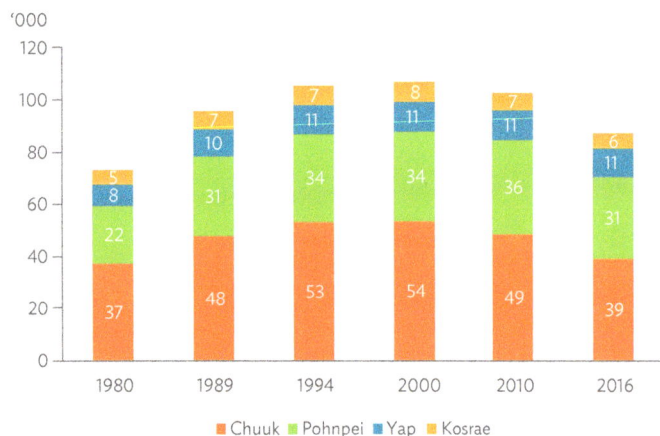

Sources: FSM Statistics Integrated Agriculture Census 2016 and 2010 Census of Population and Housing.

Informal economy is expanding

Although the data are not entirely comparable,[3] the percentage of the population engaged in subsistence or unpaid[4] employment expanded from 1994 to 2016 for both genders (Figure 4). While paid employment expanded slightly from 2000 to 2016 (from 17% to 20% for males; from 9% to 13% for females), the increase was slower compared with the increase in unpaid employment and "not in labor force."[5] Although the percentage of women not in labor force in 2016 (35%) was lower compared with 1994 (40%), it increased from 30% in 2000.

Figure 4: Federated States of Micronesia Labor Market Participation

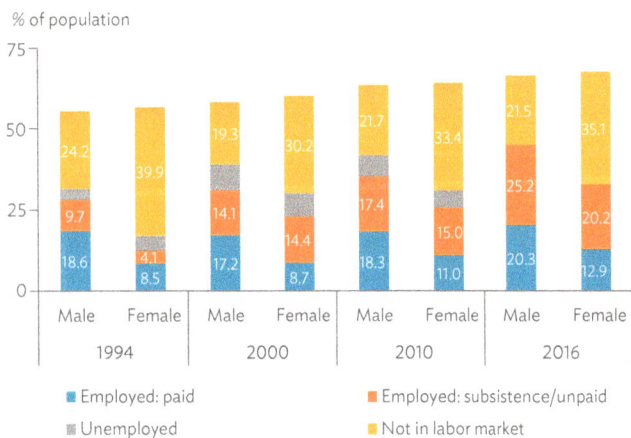

Note: Not shown in the figure are children (aged below 15) to complete 100% of population. The 2016 census does not identify the unemployed, making comparison with previous year difficult.
Sources: FSM Statistics Integrated Agriculture Census 2016 and 2010 Census of Population and Housing.

The number of people with paid jobs decreased from 15,131 in 2010 to 14,552 in 2016; while those employed but unpaid increased from 16,658 in 2010 to 19,866 in 2016 (Figure 5). Of those in paid jobs in 2016, 62% are males while 38% are females, with the ratio almost unchanged from 2010. For those in unpaid employment, 44% are females while 56% are males. The gap between the number of paid versus unpaid workers has widened since 2000, with the rapid increase in unpaid workers.

Figure 5: Federated States of Micronesia Number of Employed Workers

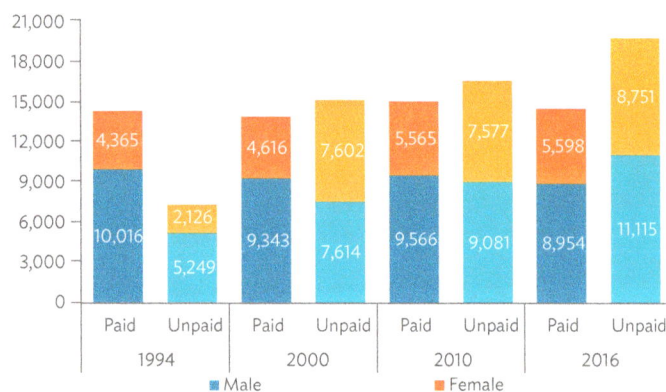

Sources: FSM Statistics Integrated Agriculture Census 2016 and 2010 Census of Population and Housing.

Among the states, Pohnpei's labor market structure was most like the national average (Figure 6). Although wide variation was observed, paid employment was consistently smaller compared with those not in the labor market. Paid employment was highest in Yap (24.9% of the population) and lowest in Chuuk (9.9%). Unpaid employment was highest in Chuuk (28.6%) and lowest in Kosrae (7.8%). Kosrae has the biggest proportion of the population not in the labor force (36.7%), while Yap has the lowest (25.7%).

Figure 6: Federated States of Micronesia Labor Market Status, by State in 2016

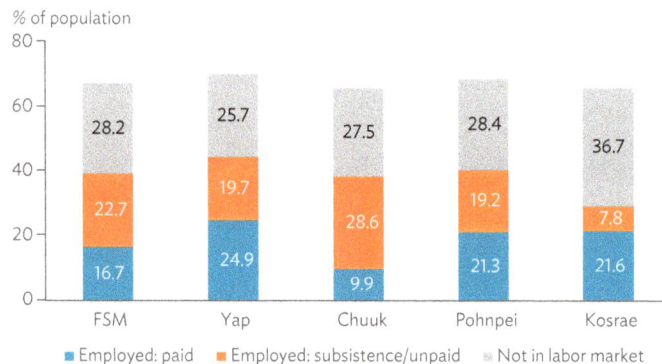

FSM = Federated States of Micronesia
Note: Not shown in the figure are children (aged below 15) to complete 100% of population.
Source: FSM Statistics Integrated Agriculture Census 2016.

Women are largely responsible for unpaid care duties

The percentage of women not in the labor force is significantly higher relative to men across all states. Nationally, about 35% of women are not in the labor force, compared with just 22% for men. Of those not in the labor force, about 60% of women (but only 35% of men) are involved primarily in home duties.[6]

Less than 13% of women in FSM had paid jobs in 2016, compared with 20% of men (Figure 7). Among the states, Kosrae has the highest percentage of women not in the labor force at 45%. Chuuk has the lowest rate of paid employment for women at less than 8%, with 20% in Yap. With paid and unpaid workers combined, Kosrae has the lowest employment rate for women at 23%.

One-third of women in the FSM are responsible for home duties, either outside the labor force (21%) or as unpaid family workers (12%) (Figure 8). For men, less than 11% are in a similar situation. Across all states, women are responsible for home duties at significantly higher rates than men. In Chuuk, almost 40% of women are engaged in home duties, only slightly higher than Pohnpei (34%) and Kosrae (30%). Women's responsibility for unpaid care has implications for their ability to participate in paid employment and decision-making roles. The COVID-19 crisis is increasing caring responsibilities and will have impacts on women's time, level of poverty, and employment prospects in the short, medium, and longer terms.

Women's paid jobs are largely in the services sector, most at risk from COVID-19

In terms of economic sector (and subsectors), agriculture is the biggest employer for men nationally (49%), while household employment is the biggest employer for women (38%) (Figure 9). Almost all (98%) workers in household employment and 90% of those working in agriculture are unpaid. For those in paid employment, public services (public administration, education, and health services) are the biggest employer for males and females; followed by other services (which include tourism and transport-related services) and wholesale and retail trade. Employment in public services is unlikely to be severely affected by COVID-19, but the impact on other services sectors is projected to be large (GS USA 2020). This is likely to have a disproportionate impact on women, who make up the largest percentage of employees in the hotel and restaurant, transport and shipping, and retail and wholesale trade sectors.

Figure 7: Federated States of Micronesia Labor Market Status, by Gender and State in 2016

% of population

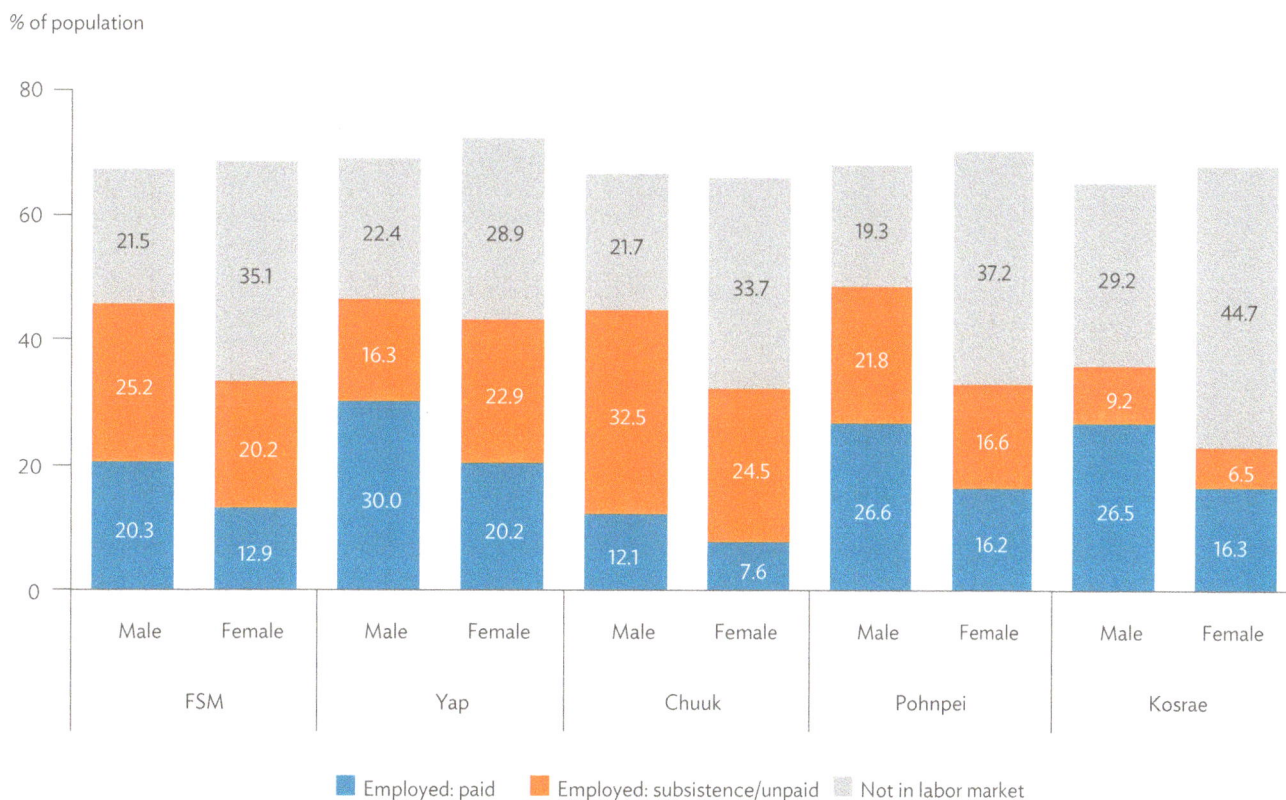

Employed: paid   Employed: subsistence/unpaid   Not in labor market

FSM = Federated States of Micronesia.
Note: Not shown in the figure are children (aged below 15) to complete 100% of population.
Source: FSM Statistics Integrated Agriculture Census 2016.

Figure 8: Federated States of Micronesia Home Duties, by Gender and State in 2016

% of population

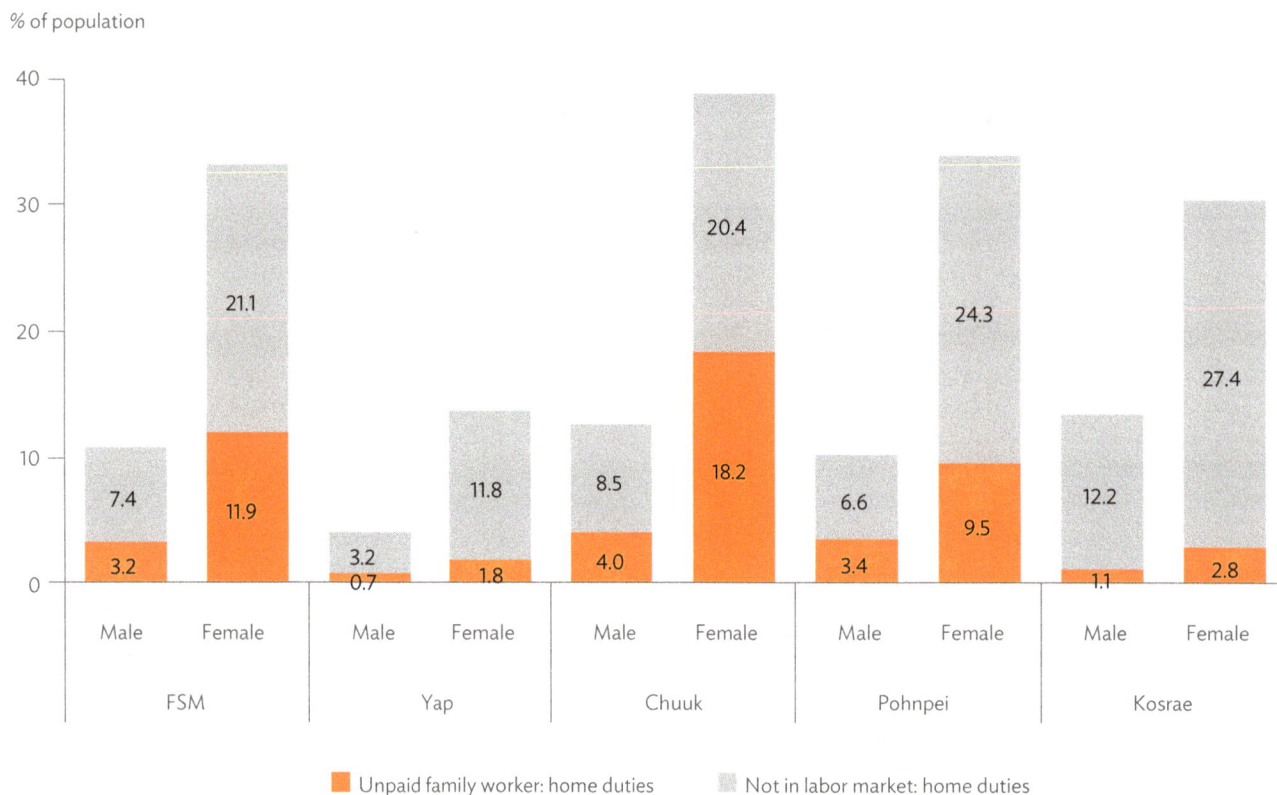

Unpaid family worker: home duties   Not in labor market: home duties

FSM = Federated States of Micronesia.
Note: Not shown in the figure are children (aged below 15) to complete 100% of population.
Source: FSM Statistics Integrated Agriculture Census 2016.

Figure 9: Federated States of Micronesia Employment, by Sector and Gender in 2016

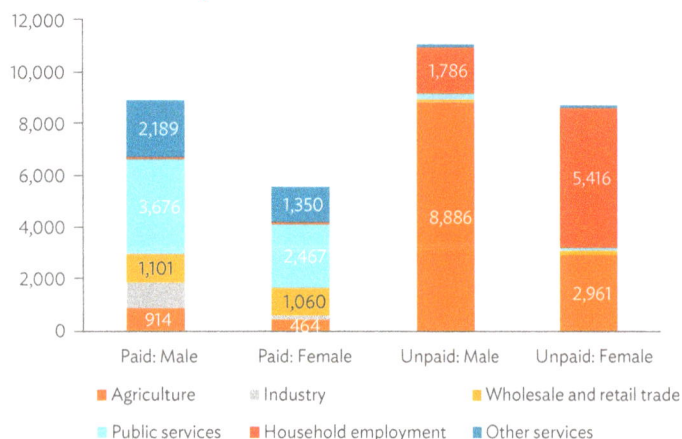

Agriculture   Industry   Wholesale and retail trade
Public services   Household employment   Other services

Notes: Agriculture includes crop production, forestry, and fisheries. Public services include public administration, education, and health.
Source: FSM Statistics Integrated Agriculture Census 2016.

Among the states, the difference between men and women is most significant in Chuuk, where almost 20% of women are in household services compared with less than 5% for men (Figure 10). Further, more than 27% of men in Chuuk are in agriculture, but less than 5% of women are in this sector. Only 1% (or less) of women in Yap and Kosrae are in household services, with agriculture being the biggest employer for women in Yap (26%), while in Kosrae, it is other services (9%). Across all states, industry plays a minor role in terms of employment, with the highest percentage seen in Yap at 4% for men.

Women are underrepresented in professional and managerial roles

In terms of occupation, the percentage of people classified as managers and professionals is relatively low in the FSM, at about 6% for men and even lower for women at less than 4% (Figure 11). While the gaps are not large, the percentage of women managers and professionals is smaller compared with men in all states. Kosrae, which has the lowest employment rate for women, has the highest percentage of managers and professionals for women among

Figure 10: Federated States of Micronesia Employment by Sector, Gender, and State in 2016

% of population

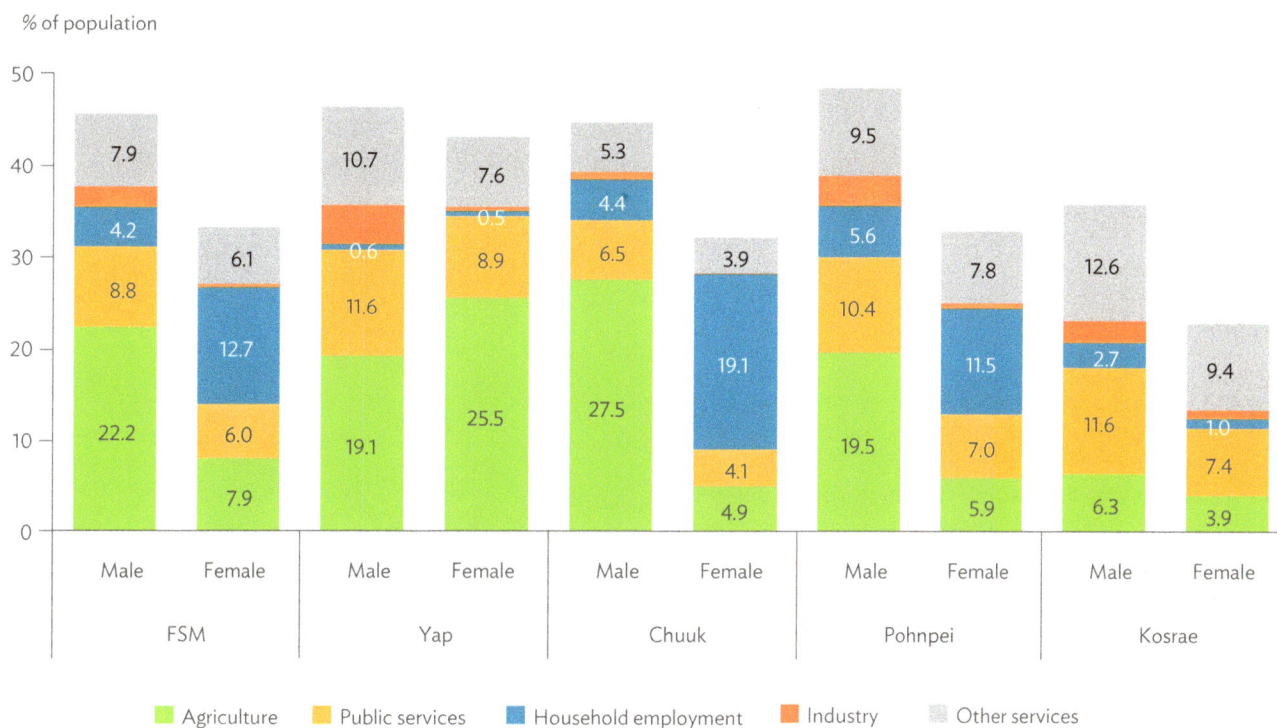

Legend: Agriculture | Public services | Household employment | Industry | Other services

FSM = Federated States of Micronesia.
Notes: Agriculture includes crop production, forestry, and fisheries. Public services include public administration, education, and health. Employment includes both paid and unpaid. Not shown in the figure are children (aged below 15) and "not in the labor force" to complete 100% of population.
Source: FSM Statistics Integrated Agriculture Census 2016.

Figure 11: Federated States of Micronesia Occupation, by Gender and State in 2016

% of population

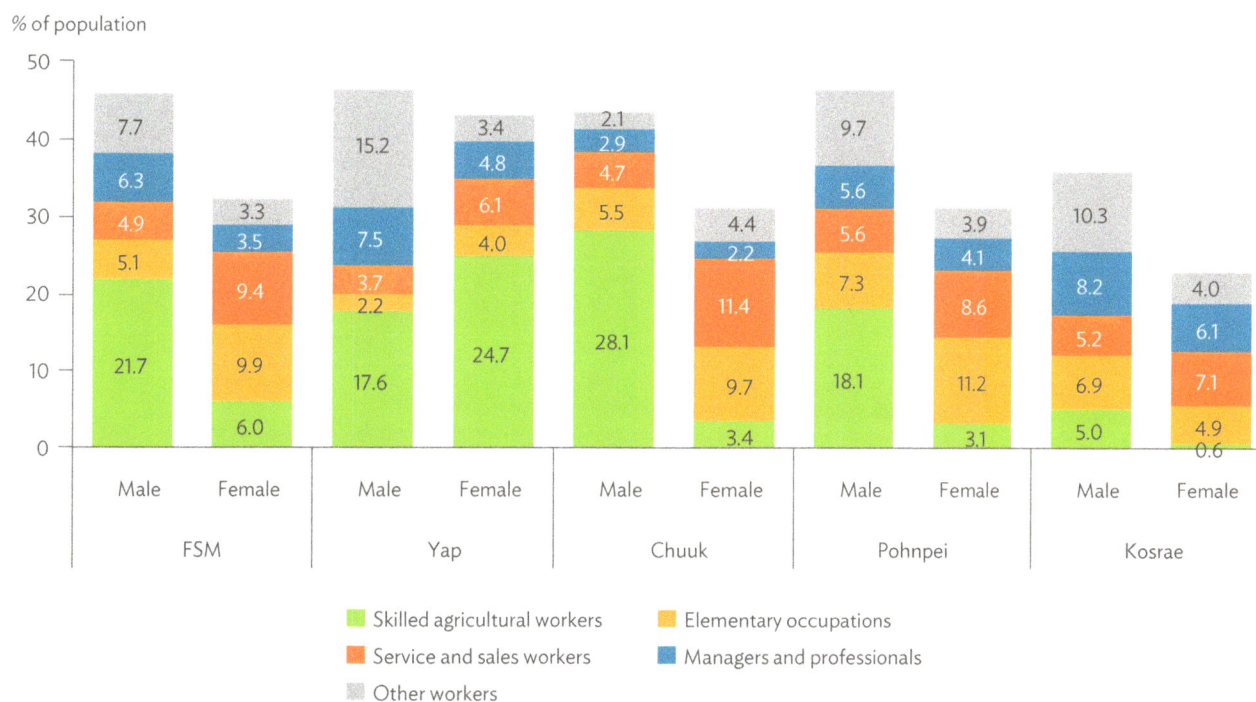

Legend: Skilled agricultural workers | Elementary occupations | Service and sales workers | Managers and professionals | Other workers

FSM = Federated States of Micronesia.
Note: Occupations in employment includes both paid and unpaid. Not shown in the figure are children (aged below 15) and 'not in the labor force' to complete 100% of population.
Source: FSM Statistics Integrated Agriculture Census 2016.

the states at 6% (although it also has the highest rate for men in that occupation). In Yap, almost 25% of female workers are skilled agricultural workers, higher than the rate for men (18%). Elementary occupations, which consist of simple and routine tasks that often require some physical effort, were the biggest employer of women nationally at about 10% and in Pohnpei at 11%. Service and sales work are also significant employers of women, at 9% nationally and 11% in Chuuk. The impacts of COVID-19, including increased caring responsibilities for women, may reduce the already small numbers of women in leadership positions.

Closing remarks

The social and economic impacts of COVID-19 are exacerbating existing inequalities and will likely challenge the progress made on gender equality in the FSM and worldwide. Even before the COVID-19 pandemic, women's participation in the paid labor force was low, but high in unpaid care. They are also less represented in senior and leadership roles. COVID-19 may accelerate these trends, with more women leaving or being forced out of the formal labor market and more women caring for household or community members. Immediate and medium term responses should account for the increased likelihood of vulnerability and poverty for women and remove barriers and create opportunities for increasing women's economic empowerment, including through safety nets for informal workers, provision of childcare options, and support for women in skilled, technical, and leadership roles.

Lead author: Prince Cruz, with inputs from Mairi Macrae

Endnotes

[1]   With the population decline observed from 2000 to 2010 reversed with the increase in 2014, projections are made assuming a continuous increase in population. Projections include FSM Statistics 103,744 in 2015; The Pacific Community (SPC) 104,380 in 2016; and Graduate School USA 103,057 in 2016.

[2]   As part of the Compact of Free Association with the United States, FSM citizens can freely move and work in the United States and its territories.

[3]   The unemployed were not specifically identified in the 2016 IAC. Around one-third of respondents in the 2014 HIES was classified as "unidentified," making comparison with other years more difficult. These data limitations also make the calculation of the labor force participation rate not comparable.

[4]   Unpaid employment includes (i) producing goods for own and/or family consumption (self-employed); (ii) unpaid family workers (family business/ plantation); (iii) unpaid family worker, help with duties inside (washing, cooking, cleaning, etc.) and outside (gardening, maintaining lawn, etc.); and (iv) volunteer work (community, church, etc.) (FSM Statistics 2019).

[5]   Not in labor force are those who are not working (paid or unpaid) and are not looking for work. They include students (part time or full time), retired individuals, and those with home duties.

[6]   DHSA (2014) explores some of the historical and cultural reasons for this.

References

Federated States of Micronesia (FSM) Statistics. 2019. *Integrated Agriculture Census 2016*. Palikir.

Government of the Federated States of Micronesia Department of Health and Social Affairs (DHSA). 2014. *A prevalence study on violence against women*. Palikir.

Graduate School USA (GS USA). 2020. Assessing the Impact of COVID-19 on the Federated States of Micronesia Economy. *Economic Monitoring and Analysis Program (EconMAP) Technical Note*. https://pitiviti.org/news/wp-content/uploads/downloads/2020/06/FSM_EconImpact_COVID-19_June2020_Web.pdf.

International Organization for Migration (IOM). 2016. *Migration in the Federated States of Micronesia: A Country Profile 2015*. Geneva.

Social protection and COVID-19 in the Pacific: economic inoculation to mitigate the impacts of the pandemic

Nine months after the World Health Organization declared the coronavirus disease (COVID-19) a pandemic, the peoples of ADB's Pacific developing member countries (DMCs) have been largely protected from the contagion and associated deaths reported in many parts of the world. The prompt action of governments in the Pacific to close the ports of entry to their territories and the inherent geographical remoteness of the island countries were crucial in controlling the spread of the virus in the subregion. Although these countries were spared from the direct health impacts of the pandemic, the containment measures have affected key sectors of the economy. For tourism-dependent countries, travel restrictions have become a bane to their services sector. The virtually zero tourist arrivals for the past several months have led to significant drops in business and government revenues. Meanwhile, a combination of stricter controls on trade and economic lockdowns overseas has reduced exports and been a huge blow to exporting island countries. Restricted movements have also caused delays in infrastructure projects in some of these countries that rely on foreign consultants and engineers, as well as imported construction equipment.

The pandemic has painted a bleak outlook for these countries, reflecting their lack of diversification, limited capacity, and remoteness. Overall, ADB (2020d) projects the Pacific subregional economy to contract by 6.1% in 2020. Most severe impacts of contraction are expected in the Cook Islands, Fiji, Palau, and Vanuatu (Figure 1).

Figure 1: Impact of COVID-19 on Full-Year 2020 Gross Domestic Product Growth Forecasts in the Pacific

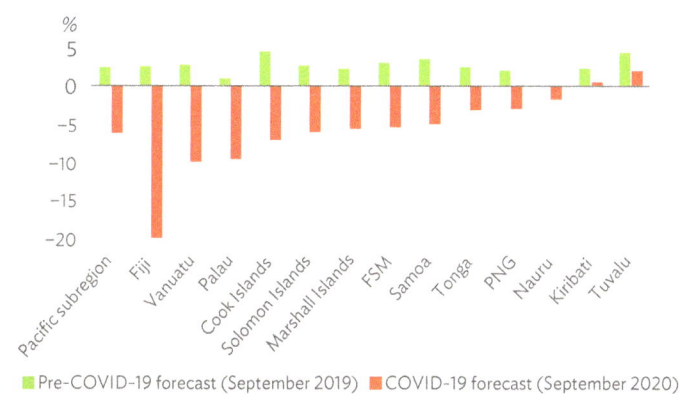

Pre-COVID-19 forecast (September 2019) COVID-19 forecast (September 2020)

ADB = Asian Development Bank, FSM = Federated States of Micronesia, PNG = Papua New Guinea.
Notes: Growth is based on fiscal years: end on 30 June for the Cook Islands, Nauru, Samoa, and Tonga; 30 September in the Marshall Islands, the Federated States of Micronesia, and Palau; and 31 December elsewhere. Forecast for Niue is not available.
Sources: ADB. 2020. *Asian Development Outlook 2020 Update: Wellness in Worrying Times.* Manila and ADB 2019. *Asian Development Outlook 2019 Update: Fostering Growth and Inclusion in Asia's Cities.* Manila.

Widespread business closures, massive job losses, and, consequently, significant drop in household incomes are affecting all aspects of societies and exposing the preexisting levels of poverty and vulnerability of marginalized groups.

Heightened vulnerability amid disruptions

The economic and social disruptions from COVID-19 are disproportionately impacting the poor and vulnerable groups who have no means to recoup quickly. Even before the pandemic, poverty, social exclusion, and vulnerability were evident in the Pacific, with about one in four Pacific islanders living below national poverty lines in 2018 (PIFS 2018). Youth unemployment in 2013 averaged 23% in the region, compared with a global average of 13% (ADB Pacific Youth Council and SPC 2016). Unemployment rates are higher for women than men in the Pacific except for Niue, Solomon Islands, and Tuvalu (SPC 2017). Women's economic participation tends to be mostly in the informal sector because as many as 75%–90% of informal market vendors in the Pacific are women (PIFS 2018). They are often excluded from social insurance, making them particularly vulnerable to economic shocks.

The region's changing demographics place additional pressure on economies and societies, and could be further aggravated by COVID-19. The number of people aged 60 years or older in the Pacific was about 512,000 as of 2014, and is projected to reach 1 million by 2030 and 2 million by 2050 (UNPF 2014). At least 1.5 million Pacific islanders, or 15% of the total Pacific population, are living with some form of disability as of 2018, heavily affected by the high rates of diabetes-related amputations and blindness,[1] plus an aging population (PIFS 2018, SPC 2016). The Pacific has the highest incidence of noncommunicable diseases, such as diabetes and its high-risk factors combined with relatively low access to prevention and treatment,[2] that further aggravates the vulnerability of the population.[3] All these have implications for labor productivity, health-care expenditures, and increased pressure on traditional and formal social protection systems. Inadequate delivery of basic services and inability to access social support from friends and family during the pandemic could also lead to abandonment and neglect, and further predispose these vulnerable groups to serious health conditions. Even without COVID-19, the Pacific must still contend with the double burden of malnutrition with high prevalence of stunting in children under 5 years and high rate of overweight and obesity mostly among children over 5 years and adolescents.[4] The poorest and most marginalized communities are more at risk to the threats of food shortages and malnutrition because of COVID-19 impacts on food supply.

Social protection as a vital component of COVID-19 response

In recognition of the economic and other problems resulting from the pandemic, governments in the subregion have provided much-needed stimulus to their respective economies and assistance to their peoples affected by the pandemic. Pacific DMCs are on average allocating 28.9% to social protection to assist the most vulnerable groups. (Figure 2). Support to businesses, particularly in the tourism sector, is the second priority with a share of 21.3%. This is followed by government spending on health preparedness measures (14.8%), food security (8.5%), and infrastructure spending (4.7%). Despite best efforts to provide a clearer categorization of the response programs, an average of 21.8% of spending is classified as "others." Six of the 13 Pacific DMCs included in this assessment have made social protection their top expenditure priority, with only one country reporting to have no amount allocated for it.

Figure 2: How Pacific Countries Allocated Their COVID-19 Response Packages

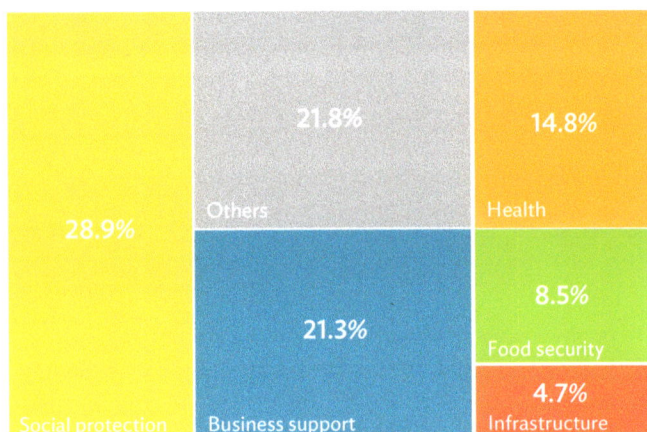

Sources: Asian Development Bank estimates using data from COVID-19 response packages and budget documents of Pacific developing member countries.

Governments employ varying approaches on their implementation of social protection measures with labor market and social assistance programs jointly accounting for an average of 23.4% of response packages (Figure 3). Meanwhile, the modest share of social insurance, at only 5.8%, reflects the narrow coverage of the formal system across the Pacific and its inability to provide immediate economic relief to the poor, vulnerable, and those in the informal sector. The Cook Islands, Niue, Solomon Islands, and Vanuatu concentrated on labor market programs as their main social protection measure, while the Federated States of Micronesia (FSM), the Marshall Islands, Papua New Guinea (PNG), Samoa, Tonga, and Tuvalu relied heavily on social assistance measures to reach their target beneficiaries. Meanwhile, Fiji and Palau mobilized their social insurance systems to provide most of their direct assistance to affected citizens. Some of the social protection programs pursued by many of these island countries are discussed in more detail below:

Figure 3: Share of Social Protection Measures in COVID-19 Response Packages

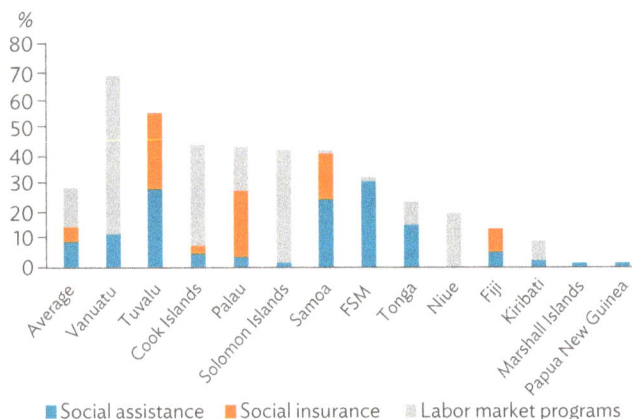

COVID-19 = coronavirus disease, FSM = Federated States of Micronesia.
Notes: Food security was not included in the chart given the complexity of disaggregating it from the social protection programs of countries. Several schemes under social assistance and labor market programs include food security.
Nauru has several existing social protection programs funded by their annual fiscal budget. Although there is no separate allocation indicated in their COVID-19 response package, they increased their financing for these programs in the 2020–2021 fiscal budget.
Sources: Asian Development estimates using data from COVID-19 response packages and budget documents of Pacific developing member countries.

Wage subsidy and unemployment support schemes. In response to COVID-19, most Pacific countries have embarked on unemployment support schemes, either through cash transfers or temporary unemployment programs. Government support also came in the form of reduction or temporary suspension of contribution payments to provident funds, special permission to withdraw from the provident fund, periodic unemployment payment support, and wage subsidies to keep businesses afloat. Countries such as the Cook Islands, Fiji, the FSM, Kiribati, Palau, and Samoa implemented cash transfers to workers whose employment has been terminated, suspended, or reduced as a result of COVID-19. Alternative temporary unemployment schemes, especially for self-employed individuals and foreign workers, are also available and administered by the government and nongovernment organizations (NGOs). To avoid dependency, receipt of unemployment assistance for more than 1 month will require proof that individuals are looking for a job. Samoa and Tuvalu have provided universal cash transfers to all citizens owing to their national policies that no one should be left behind, with Tuvalu providing a monthly cash payout to all citizens of $28 per person per month for the entire duration that the country is in a state of emergency. Frontline health workers are also eligible to receive risk benefits in the form of cash assistance in these countries.

Targeted intervention to low-income households and vulnerable groups. Countries including the Cook Islands, Fiji, the FSM, Samoa, and Tonga have considered additional assistance for poor households and vulnerable groups, such as the older persons, people with disability, and households headed by women. An estimated 10,000 smallholder farmers and poor rural households are receiving support from the Government of PNG to purchase seedlings or home gardening kits, or to manage threats to plant and animal health. The aim is to help them sustain their crop and livestock production, and thus prevent income losses from COVID-19-induced disruptions to economic activities. Samoa has provided financial assistance to welfare NGOs to avoid disruption of services to vulnerable groups and capitalize on their existing implementation mechanisms. The Cook Islands, Kiribati, Samoa, and Vanuatu also supported schools and students for continued access to education. Particularly, students in Vanuatu are exempted from fees of up to $359 per student in 2020.

Expanded social protection mechanisms. In the face of prolonged economic hardship, the Cook Islands, Fiji, Palau, and Samoa have expanded their existing social protection programs to provide additional assistance to their citizens. In the Cook Islands, a one-off payment of $250 is provided to pensioners and existing beneficiaries of caregiver, destitute, and infirm welfare payment schemes; and a child benefit payment of $63 is provided for each 2 weeks that school holidays are extended. In Fiji, temporary additional cash payments are provided to the existing beneficiaries of the Disability Allowance, Poverty Benefit, and Care and Protection Allowance schemes. Palau is expanding the targeted beneficiaries under its existing lifeline utility program for the poor households, which subsidizes 150 kilowatt-hours of electricity and 5,000 gallons each of water supply and wastewater services per household. This utility program now covers COVID-19-affected workers and their households, who may not be previously entitled to this assistance. Meanwhile in Samoa, pensioners will receive increased pensions for 1 year and a one-off payment of $111.

Labor-market programs/cash for work programs. Part of the short term economic stimulus program of Solomon Islands is its engagement of women and youth to monitor price control regulations in shops and other business activities, while planned medium term infrastructure projects included in its response package will provide longer work engagement opportunities to affected workers. Meanwhile, the Government of Vanuatu's employment stabilization payment reimbursed businesses that were affected by COVID-19 up to $256 per employee each month for 4 months. This program, which ended in September, helped workers retain their jobs despite the economic downturn. In Palau, the government is funding temporary employment schemes in the public sector and NGOs. The Cook Islands is providing a cash allowance to businesses if at least 75% of their employees completed trainings, to encourage them to upskill their workers, and training allowances of $206 per week to employees and $100 per week for part-time employees for up to 3 months. Free courses at tertiary training institutes are also available to residents of the Cook Islands. Short term paid trainings on hospitality and services sectors are available in Samoa, with an allowance of $37 for up to 4 weeks.

Focus on agriculture and food security. Food security is an important part of social protection, especially in the Pacific where most countries depend heavily on imported food items. For example, the Government of Nauru is providing additional funding to Nauru Airlines, ship leasing, and port maintenance to mitigate food supply insecurity by ensuring uninterrupted air and sea services. PNG is undertaking nationwide food security activities, including distribution of food since April. Samoa has allocated $1.3 million to promote local agriculture and fisheries, with a portion of the funding being channeled to commercialize local value-added agricultural processes. Vanuatu will also support increased production and marketing of copra, kava, cocoa, and other commodities through price subsidies and transport assistance from farms to urban centers. An estimated 31,650 households, mostly smallholder farmers, are engaged currently in cash crop production and could benefit from this support (Vanuatu National Statistics Office 2017).

Sustaining protection beyond the pandemic

The pandemic has highlighted the important role of social protection systems in providing relief to vulnerable groups in the face of crisis. However, higher spending on these measures, coupled with lower government revenues because of the economic downturn, is expected to translate to wider fiscal deficits. Fiscal deficits in Pacific DMCs are projected to be 1.4–33.4 percentage points higher compared with pre–COVID-19 projections. The latest average forecast for 2020 in Pacific DMCs is a deficit equivalent to 6.1% of GDP against a deficit of 1.2% prior to COVID-19. Without additional external financing, these countries will be forced to make significant cutbacks in other expenditures or to add considerably to public debt.

The sudden spike in social protection spending is partly indicative of the limited coverage of the preexisting programs in the Pacific. Broader social assistance programs that target the vulnerable remain underdeveloped. Although continued spending on the COVID-19-induced social protection schemes is fiscally unsustainable in the long run, governments can focus on maintaining targeted programs that consider medium term to long term outcomes that would promote poverty reduction and resilience of the poor and vulnerable groups. Governments should allocate resources in activities that will help these groups survive and equip them with skills that will be vital to their economic mobility and social welfare. The pandemic has highlighted the vulnerability of informal workers to shocks. With many of the workers in the subregion being in the informal sector, implementing reforms for a more inclusive and shock-responsive social protection to respond effectively to any types of crises should be prioritized.

Lead authors: Ninebeth Carandang and Noel Del Castillo

Endnotes

[1] According to this report, 69% of people with diabetes have retinopathy and 11% have diabetes-related amputations in some Pacific countries.

[2] Diabetes rates in some countries are 15.6% in Fiji, 19.0% in Tonga, and 24.3% in Samoa. This is much greater than the estimated 10% global prevalence (Tukuitonga 2016).

[3] The average noncommunicable disease mortality rate and adult obesity rate are substantially higher among Pacific DMCs compared with the world rates. Average noncommunicable disease mortality rate in Pacific DMCs is at 25.8% as against the world average of 18.3%; average adult obesity rate in Pacific DMCs is at 43.8% compared with the world average at 13.1% (Cruz 2020).

[4] Nauru, the Marshall Islands, Solomon Islands, Tuvalu, and Vanuatu have high prevalence of stunting in children under 5 years old; while the Cook Islands, the FSM, Fiji, Kiribati, Niue, Nauru, Palau, the Marshall Islands, Samoa, Tonga, and Tuvalu has high rate of overweight and obesity among children over 5 years of age and adolescents.

References

COVID-19 response-related documents:

ADB. 2020a. *Report and Recommendation of the President to the Board of Directors: Proposed Countercyclical Support Facility Grant to the Federated States of Micronesia for the Health Expenditure and Livelihoods Support Program.* Manila.

ADB. 2020b. *Report and Recommendation of the President to the Board of Directors: Proposed Policy-Based Grant to the Kingdom of Tonga for the Strengthening Macroeconomic Resilience Program.* Manila.

ADB. 2020c. Report and Recommendation of the President to the Board of Directors: Proposed Countercyclical Support Facility Loan to Papua New Guinea for the COVID-19 Rapid Response Program. Forthcoming.

Government of the Cook Islands. 2020. *Cook Islands Economic Response to COVID-19.* Avarua.

Government of Fiji. 2020. *Economic and Fiscal Update Supplement to the COVID-19 Response Budget Address.* Suva.

Government of Kiribati. 2020. *National COVID-19 Preparedness and Response Plan.* Tarawa.

Government of Nauru. 2020. *Republic of Nauru 2020-21 Budget and Estimates of Revenue and Expenditure.* Yaren.

Government of Niue. 2020. *Niue's Economic Response to COVID-19 Briefing Paper.* Alofi.

Government of Palau. 2020. *The Coronavirus Relief One-Stop Shop Act or CROSS Act.* Republic of Palau Public Law 10-56. Koror.

Government of the Marshall Islands. 2020. *RMI Coronavirus (COVID-19) Preparedness and Response Plan.* Majuro.

Government of Samoa. 2020. *Second Supplementary Budget Address 2019/2020.* Apia.

Government of Solomon Islands. 2020. *Economic Stimulus Package to Address the Impacts of the COVID-19 Pandemic.* Honiara.

Government of Tuvalu. 2020. *National COVID-19 Taskforce Talaaliki Plan.* Funafuti.

Government of Vanuatu. 2020. *Post-Disaster Needs Assessment TC Harold & COVID-19.* Port Vila.

Other references

ADB. 2019. *Asian Development Outlook 2019 Update: Fostering Growth and Inclusion in Asia's Cities.* Manila.

ADB. 2020d. *Asian Development Outlook 2020 Update: Wellness in Worrying Times.* Manila.

ADB, Pacific Youth Council, and the Pacific Community (SPC). 2016. *Improving Employment Opportunities for Youth in the Pacific Fragile and/or Conflict-Affected Situations: Workshop on Skills Development for Decent Work in the Pacific—Proceedings.* Suva (10–13 May).

Cruz, P. 2020. COVID-19 and the Pacific. *Pacific Economic Monitor.* July.

Pacific Islands Forum Secretariat (PIFS). 2018. *First Quadrennial Pacific Sustainable Development Report 2018: Executive Summary.* Suva.

SPC. 2017. Women's Economic Empowerment in the Pacific. Regional Overview. Prepared by the Pacific Community for the 13th Triennial Conference of the Pacific Women and the 6th Meeting of Ministers of Women.

SPC. 2016. *Pacific NCD Summit: Translating Global and Regional Commitments into Local Action—Summary Report.* Tonga (20–22 June).

Tukuitonga, C. 2016. Diabetes Remains Major Health Challenge in the Pacific. *Development Policy Blog.* 26 October. https://devpolicy.org/diabetes-remains-major-health-challenge-pacific-20161026/.

United Nations Population Fund (UNPF). 2014. *Population Ageing in the Pacific Islands: A Situation Analysis.* Suva.

Vanuatu National Statistics Office. 2017. *2016 Post TC Pam Mini Census Report.* Port Vila.

Cost-effectiveness of a COVID-19 vaccine in the Pacific: a preliminary analysis

On 30 January 2020, the World Health Organization (WHO) declared the novel coronavirus disease (COVID-19) outbreak as a public health emergency of international concern. Globally, there have been more than 54.7 million confirmed positive cases with more than 1.3 million deaths because of the disease. In the Pacific, there have been 655 confirmed cases across four ADB developing member countries (DMCs), with 9 reported deaths, as of 17 November 2020. Pacific countries continue to exert considerable efforts and incur substantial costs to prevent the entry of COVID-19 through imposing travel restrictions while mitigating the pandemic's effects on their economies.

Given their fragile health systems, full reopening of Pacific economies to international travelers will most likely have to wait until an effective COVID-19 vaccine becomes widely available. This policy brief presents a preliminary cost-effectiveness analysis of introducing a COVID-19 vaccine across four Pacific DMCs—Samoa, Tonga, Tuvalu, and Vanuatu—highlighting significant benefits from supporting the procurement of COVID-19 vaccines and investments to strengthen and prepare the existing immunization programs and health systems for its rollout, which can apply to other countries in the subregion as well.

Health sector context

Across these four countries, health care is generally free—apart from small user fees in Samoa and Vanuatu—and out-of-pocket expenditures are relatively low compared with the region and globally. The provision of health services is characterized by low utilization of health facilities and difficulties in access to care, particularly because of geographical constraints and high transport costs. High reliance on development partner support persists in many areas, including human resources, vaccines, and specialist services. Capacity for offering some diagnostic and specialist services is limited, in some cases necessitating the use of expensive overseas treatment schemes.

Despite uncertainties in coverage rates, immunization services are relatively strong across all countries, with generally high routine immunization coverage despite geographic challenges. However, Samoa has experienced declining coverage since 2018 after the unfortunate death of two children because of mishandled application of the measles-mumps-rubella vaccine. This resulted in loss in community confidence in vaccines, and the Ministry of Health decided to stop all immunizations until the cause was identified. Coverage in Vanuatu has also been generally static. Thus, there is potential to further strengthen routine immunization services through additional training, policy development, supportive supervision, and community engagement. In Samoa, further engagement with the community is required to build confidence in vaccines again. The country has invested heavily in community engagement to increase immunization awareness and sensitization to key messages to increase receptivity and decrease hesitancy since the measles epidemic of 2019.

COVID-19 impacts

Although there are very few, if any, positive cases reported in Samoa (2), Tonga (0), Tuvalu (0), and Vanuatu (1), the pandemic has necessitated intensified preparedness measures. This has resulted in increased workload on health workers for disease surveillance and testing, realigned prioritization of health managers for COVID-19 response, initial stockouts of infection control supplies and personal protective equipment, and disruptions to routine essential services including outreach services that are essential for maintaining primary health care. Countries have now focused on resuming and sustaining routine health services, while remaining vigilant for possible entry of the disease if borders are reopened.

Preparing for a COVID-19 vaccine

Because of their small population sizes, Pacific DMCs have weak individual purchasing power and weak capacity to procure vaccines independently. Given the strong global demand for a COVID-19 vaccine, which will possibly be available in 2021, Pacific DMCs will be better placed to pool demand through the global procurement facility, or COVAX facility, to ensure access. Pooled procurement will enable countries to negotiate lower prices and secure limited allocations at an early stage, while allowing for more efficient provision of regional supply and logistics management, planning and procurement, monitoring and quality assurance, and emergency stockpiles.

Pacific DMCs will also need to prepare their health systems to safely introduce the vaccine. This will require extended training for vaccinators, as well as for health managers on micro-planning to target vulnerable and high-risk populations. Risk behavior communication on infection prevention and control, along with expanded community engagement to sensitize the communities on the COVID-19 vaccine strategy and minimize potential vaccine hesitancy or misinformation will also need to be undertaken. As the COVID-19 vaccine is a new vaccine, sex-disaggregated data collection, monitoring, surveillance reporting, and support will be ideal to contribute to the global knowledge pool on vaccine rollout.

Preliminary cost-effectiveness analysis

With target COVID-19 vaccine coverage of at least 20% of the populations driven by WHO's allocation under the COVAX facility, vaccination programs across Samoa, Tonga, Tuvalu, and Vanuatu are estimated to cost a total of about $20 million. Health-care cost savings from avoided COVID-19 diagnostic testing and hospitalizations are then quantified and netted out of project costs. COVID-19 testing is estimated to cost about $19.8 per test across Samoa, Tonga, Tuvalu, and Vanuatu. The cost of avoided hospitalizations is derived from (i) the respective countries' population sizes as of 2020, along with conservative estimates of a 10% infection rate with current COVID-19 preparedness measures, and that 20% of those infected will require hospitalization; (ii) globally observed COVID-19 hospitalization costs of $34,662 per patient for low-risk populations (assumed to be 80% of total) and $45,683 per patient for high-risk or vulnerable populations (20%); (iii) government's share in hospitalization costs of 8% for Samoa, Tonga, and Vanuatu, and 13% for Tuvalu; and (iv) COVID-19 vaccine efficacy of 50%.

For Tuvalu, health-care costs are generally higher because of logistics difficulties stemming from extreme remoteness. Based on experience from ADB's regional technical assistance funding the procurement of COVID-19 test kits, personal protective equipment, and other medical supplies across Asia and the Pacific, logistics costs for delivery to Tuvalu can potentially be up to 100%–150% of the cost of goods. Further, scarcity of health-care workers available in-country because of Tuvalu's narrow population base can lead to additional costs in mobilizing overseas surge support. Thus, a cost-weighting of 250% is applied in the case of Tuvalu.

On the benefits side, averted disability-adjusted life years (DALYs)[1] are estimated using cross-country observed data on COVID-19 impacts on morbidity and mortality. Available estimates based on COVID-19 deaths as of May 2020 indicate DALYs per 1,000 population from the virus of 1.0 for Germany, 5.9 for Italy, 0.5 for Sweden, and 3.5 for the United States (US) (Mohanty et al. 2020). For Samoa, Tonga, and Vanuatu, an average of 2.7 DALYs per 1,000 population, derived from averaging above estimates in four countries, was used to quantify potentially averted DALYs per country. To account for elevated comorbidity risks in Tuvalu, which has the highest prevalence of childhood obesity (27.2%), adult obesity (51.6%), and tobacco use (48.7%) among the four countries, the highest estimated DALY per 1,000 population of 5.9 (i.e., Italy's) is applied. It is important to note here that, as the estimated DALYs per 1,000 population are from advanced economies, it is highly likely that these are underestimates in the context of the Pacific's generally heightened comorbidity risks—the average noncommunicable disease mortality rate in the Pacific is 25.8% compared with 18.3% globally—and fragile health systems (Cruz 2020). Estimated benefits are, therefore, on the conservative side.

All costs and benefits streams are expressed in 2020 US dollars and converted to economic values by excluding taxes and duties (for project costs) and applying appropriate conversion factors.[2] An incremental cost-effectiveness ratio (ICER)—measured in US dollars per DALY averted—was then calculated for the COVID-19 vaccine for each country and compared with the status quo of no vaccine.

Explicit country-specific or regional cost-effectiveness thresholds are not available. Previously, guidance for cost-effectiveness thresholds

in low-income and middle-income countries was based on GDP per capita. Interventions less than 1x GDP per capita are considered highly cost-effective, while those that fall from 1x GDP to 3x GDP per capita are considered cost-effective. It is unclear whether these thresholds accurately reflect societal willingness to pay, particularly in relation to national budgets, implying that lower benchmarks may be more in line with true willingness-to-pay thresholds.

Vaccine program costs, health-care cost savings to government, and health benefits of a COVID-19 vaccine program are used to derive COVID-19 vaccine ICERs for each country (Table 1). In the base-case analysis, a COVID-19 vaccine has ICERs that fall between 1x GDP and 3x GDP per capita in Samoa, Tonga, and Tuvalu, confirming cost-effectiveness. In the case of Vanuatu, the ICER falls below 1x GDP per capita, indicating that a COVID-19 vaccine is highly cost-effective. Therefore, introduction of a COVID-19 vaccine represents at least moderately good value for money for all four countries, assuming GDP per capita is a robust measure of societal willingness to pay.

Table 1: Cost-Effectiveness Results for a COVID-19 Vaccine

COVID-19 Vaccine	Samoa	Tonga	Tuvalu	Vanuatu
Vaccine program costs ($)	8,993,600	6,098,400	1,663,200	4,421,648
Health-care cost savings ($)	6,300,328	3,276,874	935,673	2,243,815
Hospitalizations averted (number of admissions)	4,050	2,108	233	5,926
Deaths averted (number of persons)	385	200	22	563
DALYs averted	549.3	285.9	68.4	803.8
ICER ($/DALY averted)	**4,903**	**9,869**	**10,644**	**2,710**
Population (2020)	202,506	105,401	11,664	296,314
GDP per capita ($, 2020)	3,980	4,712	3,685	2,857
ICER/GDP per capita	**1.2**	**2.1**	**2.9**	**0.9**

COVID-19 = coronavirus disease, DALY = disability-adjusted life year, GDP = gross domestic product, ICER = incremental cost-effectiveness ratio.
Source: Asian Development Bank estimates.

Given that a viable COVID-19 vaccine is not available in the market currently, there is some uncertainty in cost data. Further, as the pandemic is still ongoing but at the same time Samoa, Tonga, and Tuvalu have either remained free of the virus or recorded only a few border cases, more considerable uncertainty exists over the underlying epidemiological cost data. Varying the disease burden had important impact on results. In a low disease-burden scenario where the COVID-19 attack rate or infection rate is reduced to 5% of the population (from 10% in the baseline), ICERs will exceed 3x GDP per capita in Tonga and Tuvalu. Conversely, in a high disease-burden scenario where the attack rate is increased in 15% of the population, the COVID-19 vaccine becomes highly cost-effective with ICERs less than 1x GDP per capita in Samoa, Tonga, and Vanuatu. Further, increasing the attack rate to 16% will also result in the vaccine being highly cost-effective in Tuvalu. Improved epidemiological data can provide more certainty on vaccine cost-effectiveness.

Concluding remarks

This preliminary analysis establishes that the introduction of a COVID-19 vaccine is likely to be a cost-effective proposition not only in Samoa, Tonga, Tuvalu, and Vanuatu but also in other Pacific countries. Substantial benefits from avoided morbidity and mortality from COVID-19, risks of which are elevated because of high comorbidities in the Pacific, along with savings in testing and hospitalization costs—also inflated by the subregion's remoteness and small markets—drive this result. To achieve even better value for money, Pacific countries should harness pooled procurement platforms such as COVAX facility for an eventual COVID-19 vaccine, and the support from the United Nations Children's Fund to help secure, procure, and deliver sufficient and quality vaccines through regional cooperation.

Lead authors: Kelvin Lam and Rommel Rabanal

Endnotes

[1] Can be defined as years lost because of ill-health, disability, or premature death.

[2] Conversion factors are used to more comprehensively capture (i) opportunity costs associated with tradable, non-tradable, and labor inputs; and (ii) welfare gains stemming from project outputs from a whole-of-economy or society perspective.

References

Cruz, P. 2020. COVID-19 and the Pacific. *Pacific Economic Monitor.* July.

Mohanty, S., M. Dubey, U. Mishra, and U. Sahoo. 2020. *Impact of COVID-19 Attributable Deaths on Longevity, Premature Mortality and DALY: Estimates of USA, Italy, Sweden, and Germany.* https://www.medrxiv.org/content/10.1101/2020.07.06.20147009v1.full.pdf (accessed 13 October 2020).

Health spending and foreign aid in the Pacific

There are many similarities between the "Spanish flu" and the coronavirus disease (COVID-19) pandemics, ranging from school closures to face mask debates. So far, one deviation in their trajectories is their impact in the Pacific. Between 1918 and 1919, when the influenza pandemic swept across the world, the Pacific suffered a disproportionately[1] high mortality rate. While 3% of the world's population died of influenza, mortality reached 22% in some Pacific countries, such as Samoa. The death rate of indigenous Hawaiians was four times higher[2] than their non-indigenous counterparts.

Fortunately, the region is faring better this time around, with six of the nine COVID-19-free countries worldwide located in the Pacific.[3] However, the numerous health challenges that the region faces should not be underestimated.

On the global scale, Pacific islanders are generally[4] over-represented in rates of infectious and noncommunicable diseases. Poverty, lack of education, and limited access to health care continue to be the major drivers of this disease burden despite efforts of governments and development partners to improve the situation on the ground. Health expenditure in the Pacific varies greatly from country to country.[5] According to the World Health Organization,[6] microstates such as the Federated States of Micronesia, the Marshall Islands, Palau, and Tuvalu spend on average 14.5% of GDP on health, while larger economies, such as Papua New Guinea (PNG) and Fiji, hover at about 3%. By comparison, Australia–spends 9% of its GDP on health, and low-income countries in Southeast Asia about 6% .

In the Pacific, health expenditure is, in the main, publicly funded (Figure 1). For example, 75% of total health expenditure[7] in Kiribati and Samoa, and 66% in Fiji has been funded by their governments in 2017, with a handful of nations relying heavily on external aid financing. In PNG, for instance, 16% of the total health budget was financed externally in 2017. What is not covered by the state or foreign contributions is covered by individuals through out-of-pocket (OOP) payments. In the Pacific, OOP payments average 9% of total health expenditure. In comparison with low-income countries in Southeast Asia, where, for instance, Cambodia relies on individuals to cover OOP payments of 60%, this number may look low. Nonetheless, while low reliance on OOPs should be maintained in the Pacific to ensure even-handed access to healthcare, this low number can paradoxically arise from the challenging access to proper health services and medicine in the region. For instance, the prohibitive cost of travel—not included in the OOPs calculation—which disadvantages the majority of people living in remote outer islands and villages, can explain these low OOPs.

As a result, 10 out of 14 Pacific island countries spend $500 or less per capita per year on health services compared with the global average of about $1,000 per year.[8] Similarly, only 12 out of 21 Pacific island countries and territories—mostly those with connections to metropolitan countries like Guam or New Caledonia—have met the goal set by the World Health Organization of 4.5 health workers per 1,000 islanders.

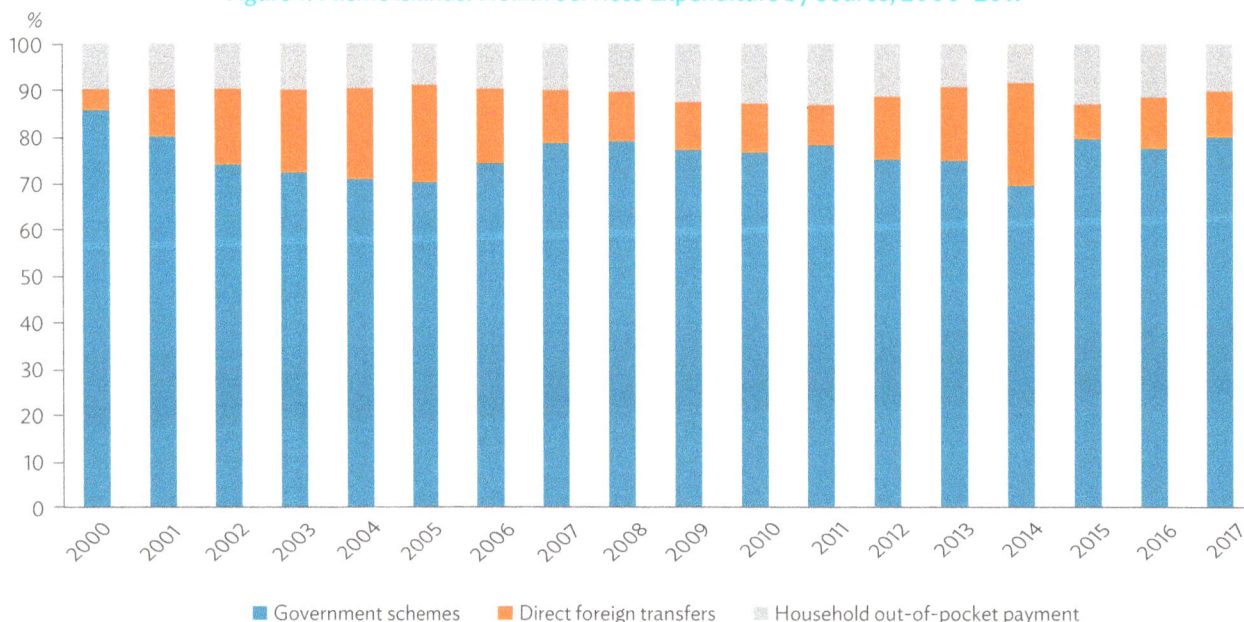

Figure 1: Pacific Islands: Health Services Expenditure by Source, 2000–2017

■ Government schemes   ■ Direct foreign transfers   ▒ Household out-of-pocket payment

Note: Pacific islands include the Cook Islands, Fiji, Kiribati, the Marshall Islands, the Federated States of Micronesia, Nauru, Palau, Papua New Guinea, Samoa, Solomon Islands, Tonga, Tuvalu, and Vanuatu.
Sources: Author's calculations, and World Health Organization - Global Health Expenditure Database 2020.

Figure 2: Pacific Islands Foreign Assistance Flows by Sector
Disbursements, 2010–2018, $ billion, current prices

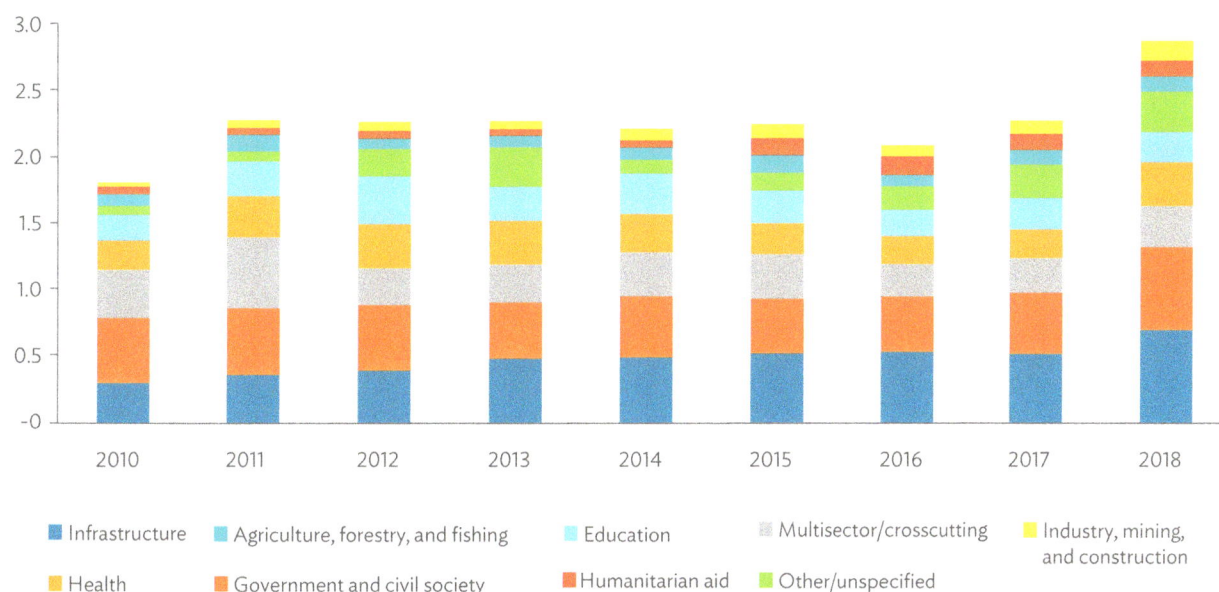

Legend:
- Infrastructure
- Agriculture, forestry, and fishing
- Education
- Multisector/crosscutting
- Industry, mining, and construction
- Health
- Government and civil society
- Humanitarian aid
- Other/unspecified

Note: Pacific islands include the Cook Islands, Fiji, Kiribati, the Marshall Islands, the Federated States of Micronesia, Nauru, Palau, Papua New Guinea, Samoa, Solomon Islands, Tonga, Tuvalu, and Vanuatu.
Source: Author's estimates using the Lowy Institute Pacific Aid Map.

Even before the COVID-19 pandemic, health systems across the Pacific were stretched, underfinanced, and, in some cases such as PNG, on the verge of collapse. Pacific leaders were prescient and responsible, locking down borders early to protect vulnerable health systems from further strain presented by COVID-19.

However, the virus has highlighted these vulnerabilities, and the current reliance on external financing of vulnerable health systems, combined with low OOP payments, makes the health financing landscape of the Pacific a unique one. With COVID-19 now surrounding the subregion, there is additional pressure on development partners to commit to additional funding.

According to the Lowy Institute Pacific Aid Map[10]—the largest and most comprehensive database of aid information ever assembled for the Pacific—health aid expenditure fluctuated between 10% and 15% of total aid expenditure in the region from 2010 to 2018 (Figure 2). There was a trend of increased health funding from 2010 to 2013, correlating with the measles[11] and Zika outbreaks, followed by a steady decrease in funding to a low period in 2016 and 2017. In 2018, ADB invested in a Health Services Sector Development Program[12] in PNG, which includes a $95 million project component that led to a 50% increase in health spending in 2018. Excluding this one-off project, health aid has been in slow but steady decline since 2012 and accounted for just 12% of all aid spent in the region over the better part of the last decade. Considering the significant health challenges that the Pacific faces, ranging from malaria to noncommunicable diseases, the funding decline is surprising. It is, however, in line with the global average since 2010—only 13% of total aid[13] was spent in the health sector in 2018.

Altogether, this support was equivalent to roughly 10% of domestic expenditure in the health sectors in Pacific countries between 2010 and 2018. These numbers suggest that health aid is of relatively minor importance, but in regard to treating endemic diseases, such as tuberculosis and HIV in PNG, foreign funding has been a game changer in the region.

Considering severe challenges, it is difficult to find a clear justification as to why health aid has not increased significantly over time.

A first potential explanation is institutional. For some major players in the health space, such as the Global Fund and Gavi, the Vaccine Alliance, arbitrary income thresholds and small populations exclude many Pacific countries from their programs. For example, because of increasing income levels, Kiribati stopped receiving Gavi immunization support in 2017, whereas a recent decision agreed that PNG[14] and Solomon Islands[15] will receive support until the end of 2021 and 2022, respectively. Vanuatu is also no longer eligible for Gavi support. Equally, financial assistance from the Global Fund to Fight AIDS, Tuberculosis, and Malaria has been decreasing since 2015. Those "graduations" from the programs of major health aid partners should be welcomed as a sign of positive development. Indeed, if aid funding is small, the departure of such organizations should not really matter. But in the Pacific, it does. Development partners often fund "big-ticket items," such as childhood vaccination programs, and HIV, tuberculosis, and malaria control on which Pacific countries rely. Yet upon departure, development partners often leave a financing gap that puts Pacific countries at risk.

A second explanation for stagnant health aid funding is that for bilateral donors, the health sector must contend with the more appealing or strategically significant sectors of governance and transport. Aid volumes in 2018 increased significantly in the Pacific, with total aid surging by 26%[16] to a record $2.8 billion, roughly 8.5% of regional GDP. Of this increase, the majority went to governance and infrastructure projects.

Those restraints put further pressure[17] on domestic health systems to find ways to spend their health dollars more efficiently.

The silver lining of the current pandemic is that it has snapped health systems back into focus. It has also revealed clear gaps in domestic health coverage in the Pacific. Domestic demand for greater health support will certainly grow in the decade to come.

The challenge that Pacific governments face is to satisfy this demand.

Historically, economic growth is the main determinant of a real increase in support for the health sector. The current crisis is likely to have a significant and disproportionate impact on health budgets across the Pacific at a time when health spending should progress the subregion toward sustainable and fit-for-purpose health systems and universal health coverage. The current economic downturn will put tremendous pressure on budgetary needs for health spending that, in many settings, is already constrained and insufficient.

Fortunately, experience of events such as the 2008 global financial crisis suggest that health services may be protected in budgetary allocations. Apart from Nauru, which experienced a dramatic boom and bust of its health expenditure over the period, health budgets in the Pacific region stayed stable during the last economic crisis. Nonetheless, maintaining previous allocation levels will not be enough in the face of the growing health funding needs resulting from COVID-19.

Foreign assistance financing options are also beginning to look increasingly uncertain, with the volume and destination of development assistance for health waning. High-income countries are currently suffering from significant economic downturns, fiscal deficits, and unprecedented levels of debt, which hamper their ability to support the Pacific, as occurred after the global financial crisis.[18] The sizeable global economic downturn has already affected the national income of development partners. As a result, those with a fixed official development assistance target of 0.7% of gross national income might see their income basis diminished, resulting in lower disbursement of aid in real terms. In addition, the economic hardship caused by the pandemic may lead to a greater number of countries seeking support from what may end up being a smaller pot. In that context, the Pacific region risks missing out on much-needed financial assistance.

Overall, the economic crisis plaguing the Pacific will further reduce the ability of their governments to finance health services, placing even more pressure on development partners to help fill the funding gap. With these budgets strapped as countries fight their own recessions, the Pacific will have to learn to do more with less.

Lead author: Alexandre Dayant, Lowy Institute

Endnotes

[1]   Wilson et al. 2005.

[2]   Schmitt and Nordyke. 1999.

[3]   Data as of 27 November 2020.

[4]   Horwood et al. 2019.

[5]   Includes the Cook Islands, Fiji, Kiribati, the Marshall Islands, the Federated States of Micronesia, Nauru, Palau, Papua New Guinea, Samoa, Solomon Islands, Tonga, Tuvalu, and Vanuatu.

[6]   World Health Organization (WHO). 2020.

[7]   WHO. 2020.

[8]   WHO. 2020.

[9]   Negin et al. 2012.

[10]   Lowy Institute. 2020.

[11]   Hagan et al. 2018.

[12]   Asian Development Bank. 2020.

[13]   Development Initiatives. 2020.

[14]   Gavi. 2020.

[15]   Gavi. 2020.

[16]   Lowy Institute. 2020.

[17]   Ruest. 2018.

[18]   OECD. 2020.

References

Asian Development Bank. 2020. Papua New Guinea: Health Services Sector Development Program. https://www.adb.org/projects/51035-001/main#project-overview

Development Initiatives. 2020. Aid Spent on Health: ODA Data on Donors, Sectors, Recipients - Factsheet, July 2020. https://devinit.org/resources/aid-spent-health-oda-data-donors-sectors-recipients/

Organisation for Economic Co-operation and Development (OECD). 2020. The Impact of the Coronavirus (COVID-19) Crisis on Development Finance. 24 June 2020. http://www.oecd.org/coronavirus/policy-responses/the-impact-of-the-coronavirus-covid-19-crisis-on-development-finance-9de00b3b/

Gavi, the Vaccine Alliance. 2020. Solomon Islands Joint Appraisal 2019. https://www.gavi.org/sites/default/files/document/2020/Solomon Islands Joint Appraisal 2019.pdf

Hagan J.E. et al. 2018. Progress Toward Measles Elimination — Western Pacific Region, 2013–2017. *Morbidity and Mortality Weekly Report 2018*. 67. 491-495. https://www.cdc.gov/mmwr/volumes/67/wr/mm6717a3.htm

Horwood, P.F., A. Tarantola, C. Goarant, M. Matsui, E. Klement, M. Umezaki, S. Navarro, and A.R. Greenhill. 2019. Health Challenges of the Pacific Region: Insights from History, Geography, Social Determinants, Genetics, and the Microbiome. *Frontiers in Immunology*. 10. 2184. https://www.ncbi.nlm.nih.gov/pmc/articles/PMC6753857/.

Lowy Institute. 2020. Pacific Aid Map. https://pacificaidmap.lowyinstitute.org/

Negin, J., A.L.C. Martiniuk, P. Farell, and T. Dalipanda. 2012. Frequency, Cost and Impact of Inter-island Referrals in the Solomon Islands. *Rural Remote Health 2012*. 12. 2096. www.rrh.org.au/journal/article/2096

Ruest, M. 2018. *Making Health Dollars Go Further in the Pacific.* https://devpolicy.org/making-health-dollars-go-further-inthe-pacific-20180628/.

Schmitt, R.C. and E.C. Nordyke. 1999. Influenza Deaths in Hawai'i, 1918–1920. *The Hawaiian Journal of History*. 33:101-117. https://evols.library.manoa.hawaii.edu/bitstream/10524/538/JL33107.pdf

Wilson, N., O. Mansoor, D. Lush, and T. Kiedzynski. 2005. Modeling the Impact of Influenza Pandemic on Pacific Islands. *Emerging Infectious Diseases*. 11(2). 347-349. https://www.ncbi.nlm.nih.gov/pmc/articles/PMC3320443/

World Health Organization. 2020. Global Health Expenditure Database. https://apps.who.int/nha/database

Nonfuel Merchandise Exports from Australia
(A$; y-o-y % change, 3-month m.a.)

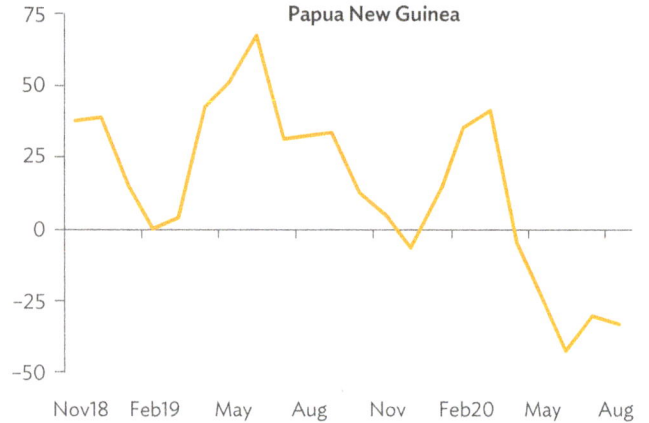

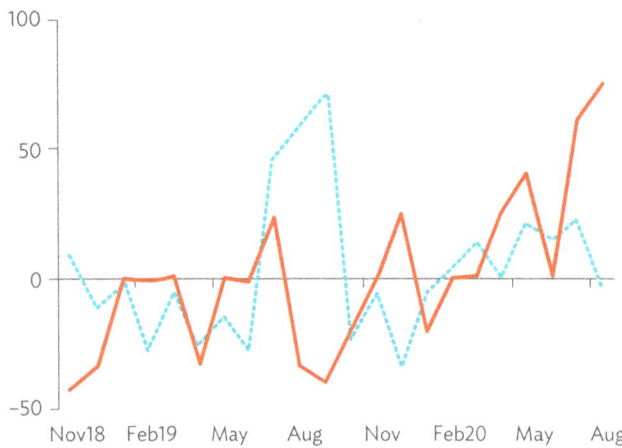

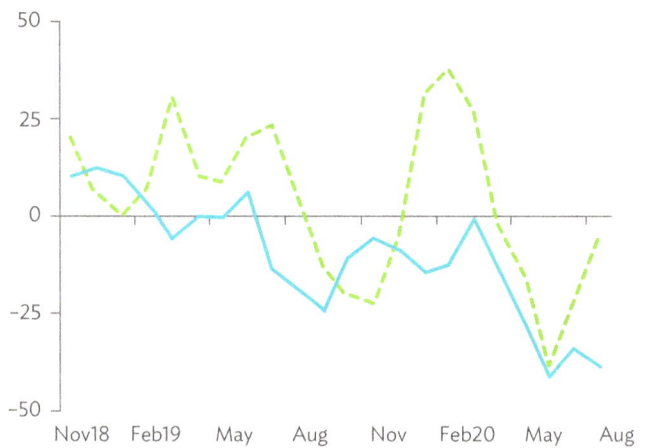

Fiji

Papua New Guinea

Kiribati   Nauru

Solomon Islands   Vanuatu

A$ = Australian dollar, lhs = left-hand scale, m.a. = moving average, rhs = right-hand scale, y-o-y = year-on-year.
Source: Australian Bureau of Statistics.

Nonfuel Merchandise Exports from New Zealand and the United States
(y-o-y % change, 3-month m.a.)

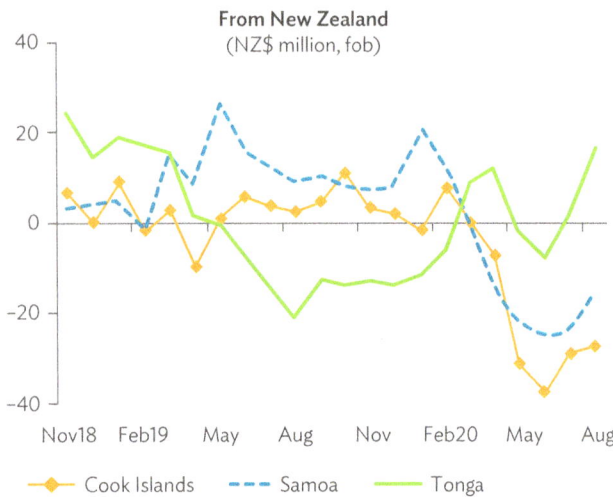

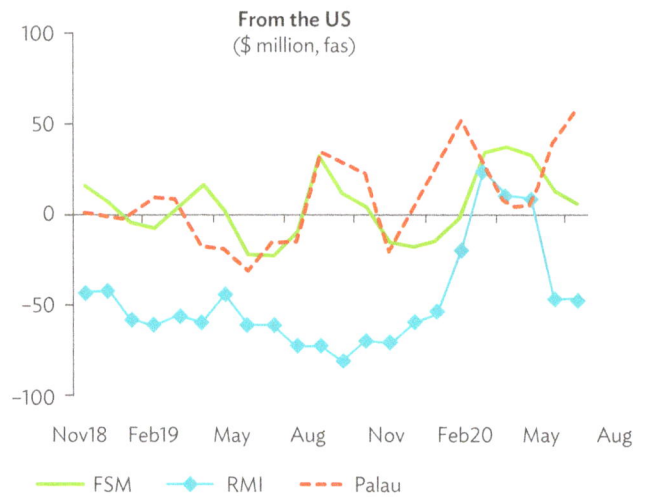

From New Zealand
(NZ$ million, fob)

From the US
($ million, fas)

Cook Islands   Samoa   Tonga

FSM   RMI   Palau

fas = free alongside, fob = free on board, FSM = Federated States of Micronesia, m.a. = moving average, NZ$ = New Zealand dollar, RMI = Republic of the Marshall Islands, US = United States, y-o-y = year on year.
Sources: Statistics New Zealand and US Census Bureau.

Diesel Exports from Singapore
(y-o-y % change, 3-month m.a.)

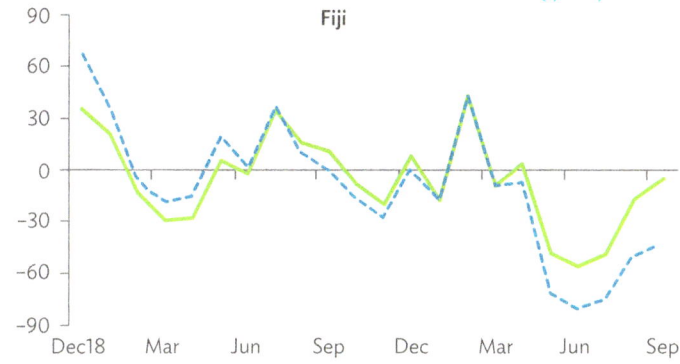

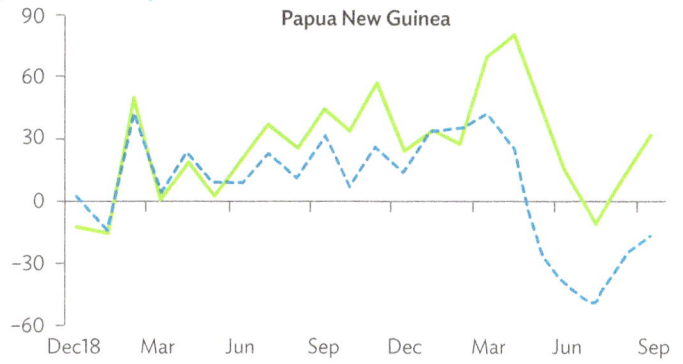

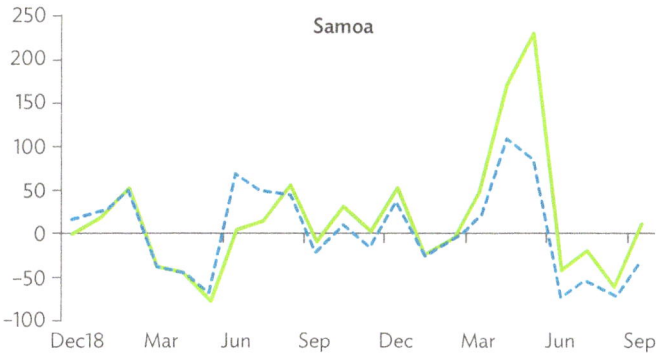

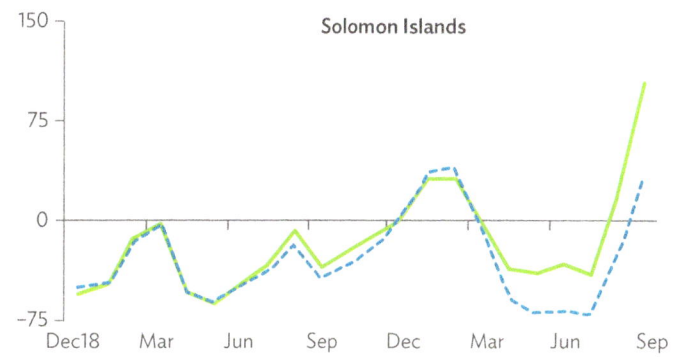

Fiji

Papua New Guinea

Samoa

Solomon Islands

—— Volumes   - - - Values

m.a. = moving average, y-o-y = year on year.
Source: International Enterprise Singapore.

Gasoline Exports from Singapore
(y-o-y % change, 3-month m.a.)

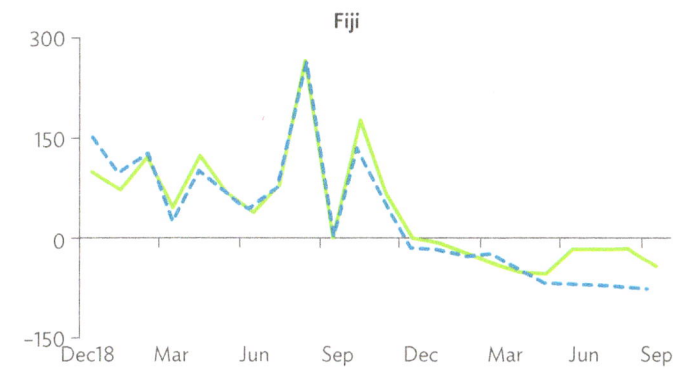

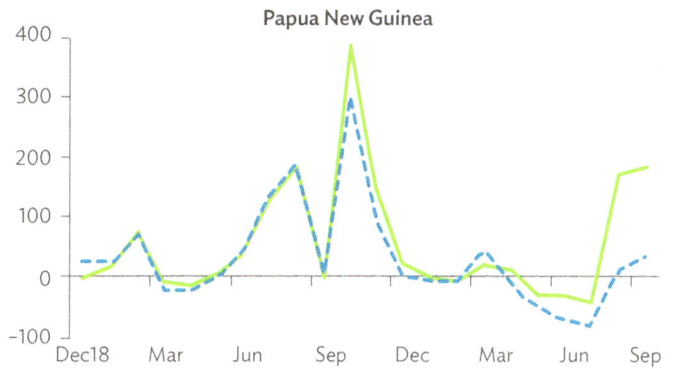

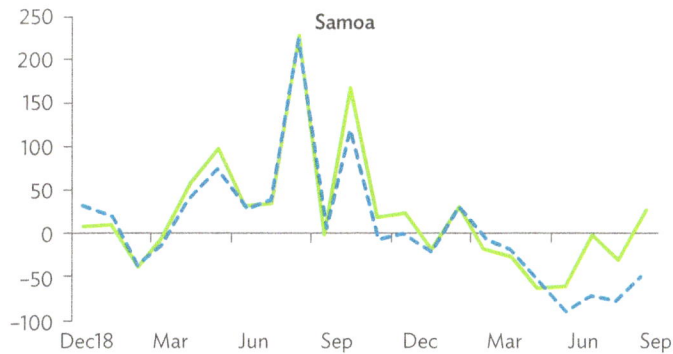

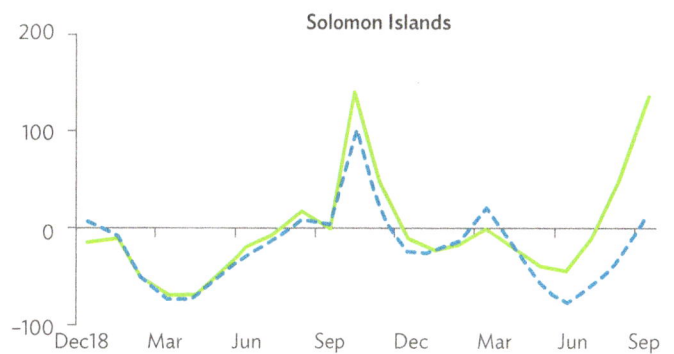

Fiji

Papua New Guinea

Samoa

Solomon Islands

—— Volumes   - - - Values

m.a. = moving average, y-o-y = year on year.
Source: International Enterprise Singapore.

Departures from Australia to the Pacific
(monthly)

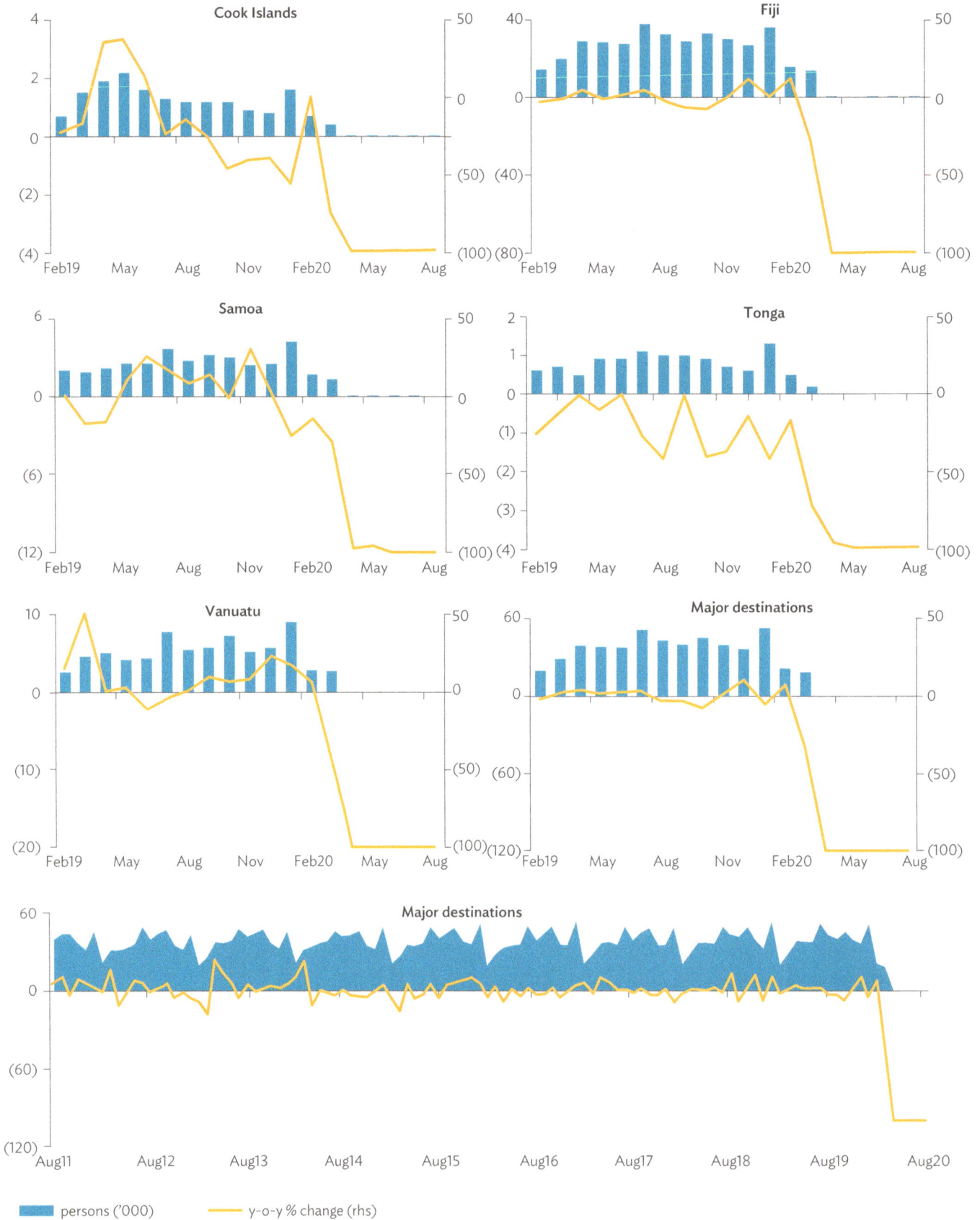

Cook Islands

Fiji

Samoa

Tonga

Vanuatu

Major destinations

Major destinations

■ persons ('000)   ── y-o-y % change (rhs)

rhs = right-hand scale, y-o-y = year on year.
Source: Australian Bureau of Statistics.

www.ingramcontent.com/pod-product-compliance
Lightning Source LLC
Chambersburg PA
CBHW040147200326
41519CB00035B/7625